You Can Experience . . .

An Authentic Life

James Emery White

WORD PUBLISHING

NASHVILLE

A Thomas Nelson Company

Published by Word Publishing, a unit of Thomas Nelson, Inc., P.O. Box 141000, Nashville, Tennessee 37214. No portion of this book may be reproduced, stored in a retrieval system, or transmitted in any form or by any means—electronic, mechanical, photocopy, recording, or other— except for brief quotations in printed reviews, without the prior permission of the publisher.

Unless otherwise indicated, Scripture quotations used in this book are from the Holy Bible, New International Version (NIV). Copyright © 1973, 1978, 1984, International Bible Society. Used by permission of Zondervan Bible Publishers.

Other Scripture references are from the following sources:

The Holy Bible, New Century Version (NCV), copyright © 1987, 1988, 1991 by Word Publishing, Nashville, Tennessee 37214. Used by permission.

The Living Bible (TLB), copyright © 1971 by Tyndale House Publishers, Wheaton, Illinois. Used by permission.

The Message (MSG), copyright © 1993. Used by permission of NavPress Publishing Group.

J. B. Phillips: The New Testament in Modern English, Revised Edition (PHILLIPS). Copyright © J. B. Phillips 1958, 1960, 1972. Used by permission of Macmillan Publishing Co., Inc.

The Good News Bible: The Bible in Today's English Version (TEV), copyright © 1976 by the American Bible Society.

The Holy Bible, New Living Translation (NLT), copyright © 1996. Used by permission of Tyndale House Publishers, Inc., Wheaton, Illinois. All rights reserved.

The Contemporary English Version (CEV), © 1991 by the American Bible Society. Used by permission.

Library of Congress Cataloging-in-Publication Data

White, James Emery, 1961–
    You can experience an authentic life / James Emery White.
        p. cm.
    Includes bibliographical references.
    ISBN 0-8499-3787-6 (tp)
        1. Spiritual life—Christianity. I. Title.
BV4501.2 .W448 2000
248.4—dc 21

00-042895
CIP

Printed in the United States of America

00 01 02 03 04 05 PHX 6 5 4 3 2 1

ALSO BY JAMES EMERY WHITE

Rethinking the Church

A Search for the Spiritual

You Can Experience a Spiritual Life

You Can Experience a Purposeful Life

Contents

Acknowledgments

My indebtedness to the teaching and writing of others is indicated on the notes page, but of particular help throughout was my friend Bill Hybels's sermon series delivered at Willow Creek Community Church in South Barrington, Illinois, as well as his book *The Laws That Liberate*. Bill's positive approach to the Ten Commandments inspired me to use them for a broad approach to a life of authenticity through obedience. Other helpful sources on the Ten Commandments included Bill and Kathy Peel's *Where Is Moses When We Need Him?* J. I. Packer's *The Ten Commandments*, and Joy Davidman's *Smoke on the Mountain*.

I am indebted to my assistant, Glynn Goble, who has demonstrated a spirit to serve with loyalty, grace, and enthusiasm. I am very grateful for her ministry. I must also mention again the good folks of Mecklenburg Community Church, who are simply the best community of people in the world. (Are we having too much fun to be legal, or what!) Their enthusiasm over our joint ten-week journey through "God's Top-Ten List" reminded me of each commandment's lasting relevance and ongoing spiritual potency.

I also want to thank the team at Word, particularly Mark Sweeney, Ami McConnell, and Jennifer Stair, for their vision and support and for helping to make each book much better *after* I write it.

As always, the greatest thanks goes to my wife, Susan, who as always made every page possible.

—James Emery White
Charlotte, North Carolina

An Opening Word

au•then•tic (ô then'tik) **adj. 1.** can be believed or accepted; trustworthy; reliable; **2.** is in fact as represented; genuine; real

In the movie *Good Will Hunting,* Robin Williams won an Oscar for his role as a psychology professor who attempts to reach out and help a headstrong, working-class genius who is failing the most basic lessons of life. Will Hunting, played by Matt Damon, begins his relationship with Williams's character by wielding his sharp wit and intellect toward the professor in an effort to wound him in his most vulnerable area—his deceased wife. Unlike other therapists who had been on the receiving end of Will's cutting tongue, Williams turns the tables in their second visit by revealing the truest, deepest nature of Will's life:

"Thought about what you said to me the other day. . . . I stayed up half the night thinking about it. [Then] something occurred to me, and [I] fell into a deep, peaceful sleep and haven't thought about you since. You know what occurred to me?"

"No," replies Will.

"You're just a kid. You don't have the faintest idea what you're talking about."

"Why, thank you," comes the sarcastic reply.

"It's all right," replies Williams. "You've never been out of Boston?"

"Nope."

From that, Williams proceeds to dissect the heart of another human being's existence.

"So if I asked you about art, you'd probably give me the skinny on every art book ever written. Michelangelo, you know a lot about him—[his] life's work, political aspirations, him and the pope, sexual orientation, the whole works, right? But I bet you can't tell me what it smells like in the Sistine Chapel. You've never actually stood there and looked up at that beautiful ceiling . . .

"If I asked you about women, you'd probably give me a syllabus of your personal favorites . . . but you can't tell me what it feels like to wake up next to a woman and feel truly happy.

"You're a tough kid. If I asked you about war, you'd probably throw Shakespeare at me, right? 'Once more into the breach, dear friend.' But you've never been near one. You've never held your best friend's head in your lap and watched him gasp his last breath looking to you for help.

"If I asked you about love, you'd probably quote me a sonnet. But you've never looked at a woman and been totally vulnerable. [Never] known someone who could level you with her eyes, feeling like God put an angel on earth just for you, [who] could rescue you

from the depths of hell. And you wouldn't know what it's like to be
her angel, to have that love for her be there forever . . . through anything . . . through cancer. And you wouldn't know about sleeping
sitting up in a hospital room for two months holding her hand
because the doctors could see in your eyes that the term *visiting
hours* doesn't apply to you.

"You don't know about real loss, because that only occurs when
you love something more than you love yourself. I doubt you've
ever dared to love anybody that much.

"I look at you—I don't see an intelligent, confident man. I see
a cocky, scared . . . kid."

Few moments in cinematic history have so eloquently captured
the nature of what it means to be a real human being. Life is not
about knowledge; it's about *experience*. Words alone are meaningless. What makes something real is living it.

This is a book about experiencing an authentic life—not just
authenticity in general, but personal, *spiritual* authenticity. To be
an authentic Christian demands more than just knowing the right
things to do; it demands the experience of the Christ-life, the following of the Christ-life. Jesus Himself said, "Why do you call me,
'Lord' . . . and do not do what I say?" (Luke 6:46). There is a
direct, inescapable link between action and authenticity. To know
is to do; to believe is to behave. But what actions should we take?
Knowing exactly what we should do to have authentic lives can be
a difficult task, for it's all too easy to miss out on what it means to
truly follow our Master Teacher.

Consider the time a small bottle of urine sat on the desk at the front of the Oxford University classroom. Sir William Osler, the eminent professor of medicine, stood before his class of eager young students in order to give them a lecture on the importance of observing details. He lifted up the bottle of urine and said, "This bottle contains a sample for analysis. It is possible, simply by tasting it, to determine the disease from which the patient suffers."

He dipped a finger into the fluid and then into his mouth.

"Now I am going to pass the bottle around. Each of you please do exactly as I did. Perhaps we can learn the importance of this technique and diagnose the case."

The bottle was passed, row by row, student to student. At each stop, a student carefully poked his or her finger into the bottle of urine, and then, bravely, into their mouth. After the bottle traveled to every person in the room, Osler took the vial, set it down, and said, "Now you will understand what I mean when I speak about details. Had you been observant, you would have seen that I put my *index* finger into the bottle but my *middle* finger into my mouth!"[1]

Osler's students learned that the key of authenticity is to do *exactly* what the master prescribes. An authentic follower moves beyond mere observation to the actual practice of what the master does. Likewise, an authentic Christian is one who has gone beyond the initial step of observation to actually *following* what the Master says. Suddenly, authenticity becomes a matter of *obedience*.

Obedience is a dirty word that conjures up images of slavery and oppression, tyranny and abuse. We've phased it out of marriage ceremonies, scrubbed it from our schools, eliminated it from the workplace, and fought—often literally—for its political extinction.

Frequently, this has been a good thing. Obedience should never be given indiscriminately, and those in authority should call for it with the utmost caution and care. When authority is abused, resistance is natural. But the idea of obedience *itself* is not negative. It's *good* to obey the laws of gravity and not step out of a twelve-story window. I *want* to obey nutritional guidelines to provide for the optimum in physical health. It was *important* that I obeyed my mother when, as a child, I made a beeline toward a street full of fast-moving cars and she commanded me to stop.

A television news camera crew was on assignment in southern Florida, filming the widespread destruction of Hurricane Andrew. Amid the devastation and debris stood a single house remaining on its foundations. The reporter approached the owner as he cleaned up his front yard.

"Sir," the reporter asked, "why is your house the only one still standing? How did you manage to escape the severe damage of the hurricane?"

"I built this house myself," the man answered. "I also built it according to the Florida state building code. When the code called for two-by-six roof trusses, I used two-by-six roof trusses. I was told that a house built according to code could withstand a hurricane. I did, and it did. I suppose no one else around here followed the code."[2]

Obedience to the right people, accompanied by appropriate boundaries and clear realities, is not only good, but it is the essence of life itself. Frederich Buechner reminds us that the common perception that to obey somebody is necessarily to do something for somebody else's sake is a tragic misunderstanding. When Jesus asks people to obey, it is for their *own* sakes.[3] If you want to enjoy the satisfaction of an authentic life, you must first learn to obey the commands of Jesus—for your own sake. An authentic Christian is an obedient Christian. If you have never joined these two ideas together, you have missed out on the nature of what it means to be real.

Walk through this with me for a moment. As Christians, we are called to transform our character into the likeness of Jesus Christ (see Rom. 8:29). Our commitment to becoming more like Christ compels us to move from merely observing His life to actually incorporating His thoughts and His actions into our own lives. An *authentic* Christian—that is, someone who genuinely seeks to become like Christ—makes a dedicated, daily, conscious effort to live the Christ-life. This can only be achieved through obedience. Anything else is contrary to our commitment as Christians and marks us as inauthentic.

But how can we obey God? This is a dilemma on two fronts. First, there is the playing field itself. If I am to obey God, what are the rules, guidelines, principles, and precepts I am to follow? Even the most tentative explorations of the Bible can leave a reader gasping for breath at the scope of God's standards for a life, with endless questions as to what counts—and what doesn't.

Without boundaries, we can find ourselves racing into situations and problems that we would have preferred to avoid. Before his death, Lewis Grizzard was a columnist for the *Atlanta Constitution*. In one of his books, he tells of something that happened one day in a town in Georgia called Young Harris.

Young Harris was a very small town—so small that they didn't have a fire department, not even a volunteer fire department. One day, a house caught fire in Young Harris, and the whole town gathered to watch it, helpless to put it out. About that time, they saw a pickup truck come over the ridge, driven by a local man by the name of Fuzz Chastain. In the truck with him were his wife, all their kids, a cousin or two, and a few aunts and uncles. Fuzz drove right to where everyone was standing, but he didn't stop. Instead, he drove that pickup truck right into the middle of the fire! He jumped out, and so did everybody else in the truck. They started beating the fire with anything they could find, even their clothes! It took them thirty minutes, but they put out every lick of that fire.

The mayor was among the admiring spectators, and he proclaimed, "This is the most courageous thing I have ever seen or heard tell of in the history of our city. Let's pass the hat for Fuzz Chastain." So they did—and the crowd raised a grand total of seventeen dollars. The mayor presented the money to Fuzz, who stood there with singed hair and torn, burnt clothes.

"Fuzz," he said, "the people of Young Harris appreciate your heroic act." He gave him the seventeen dollars and then, not knowing what else to do, asked, "So Fuzz, what are you going to do with this money?"

Fuzz thought a minute, then he answered, "Well, Mr. Mayor, I guess the first thing I ought to do is get the brakes fixed on that dang pickup so that I won't drive into any more fires!"[4]

Like Fuzz, we need to have some brakes in operation, because after you've been in a fire or two, you know they ain't fun. That's why God gave us boundaries in His Word. If we follow His guidelines, we'll know how and when to stop before our lives spin out of control.

But even when we truly desire to experience authenticity, building patterns of obedience into our lives is not exactly easy. Most of us empathize with the apostle Paul's words at the end of Romans 7: "I've tried everything and nothing helps. I'm at the end of my rope. Is there no one who can do anything for me? . . . I want to serve God with all my heart and mind, but am pulled by the influence of sin to do something totally different" (vv. 21–22 MSG).

Fortunately, when it comes to the question of *what* we are to obey, God narrowed it down to a top-ten list in the form of the Ten Commandments.[5]

Now I know when you read the words *Ten Commandments,* all kinds of ideas and images come into your mind. Like the actor Charlton Heston who played Moses in the big-screen epic of old. Or a list of legalistic, binding, archaic dos and don'ts that make you want to run for the hills. Let me make one simple request: Try to suspend all of the pop-culture images and negative ideas you have about the Ten Commandments, and accept a challenge to take a fresh look at the entire set in the way that God intended.

Because here's what they're about.

After the exodus from Egypt, God took His people aside and gave them a list of ten things that revealed His holiness and set appropriate boundaries for their lives. And people have looked to these ten statements as a road map for an authentic life of obedience to God, bringing the life God intended, ever since.

God's top-ten list isn't in the category of "doing more." We've tried enough commands calling for self-disciplined rituals and have found them impotent. Instead, these ten statements engage at the deepest level of "being more." These commands address the universal desire to be a different kind of person, an authentic person, not just someone whose behavior patterns and biblical knowledge impress the casual onlooker but do not reflect the essence of their lives.[6] As a result, these ten statements have been a compelling standard of living for generations.

Until recently.

During the last several years, the Ten Commandments have been increasingly ignored, caricatured, marginalized, and lampooned. Polls show that 80 percent of us believe in them, but very few can name as many as four of them. Even fewer feel led to investigate them for their life.[7] God has given us His top-ten list for an obedient, authentic life, but for most people, these standards are unexplored territory.

So let's begin with the first step toward an authentic life, encompassing the most foundational dynamic of all: *putting God first.*

CHAPTER 1

Putting God First

Ray Kroc, founder of the fast-food chain McDonald's, was once asked to list the three most important things in his life. His answer? "God, my family, and McDonald's."

Not bad. Only he didn't stop there. "But when I get to the office," he continued, "I reverse the order."

The first of the Ten Commandments tells us what should be the most important thing in our lives—regardless of where we are: "And God spoke all these words: 'I am the LORD your God. . . . You shall have no other gods before me'" (Exod. 20:1–3). In other words, God's first commandment is to put Him first in our lives.

Now God is not saying that there really *are* other gods you could possibly encounter and that He wants to make sure—in case any others show up—that He has a corner on the market. Few things are more clearly and emphatically taught in the Bible than the fact that there is one and only one God.

What this commandment *is* saying is that we can choose to

have something *other* than the one God be *first*. Whatever you love most, serve most, seek out most, give to the most, worship the most, and care about the most is your god.[1]

Your "god" can be your career, your bank account, the way you look, a particular position or degree, influence, power, or physical pleasure. It can even be something that is considered intrinsically good, yet you allow it to dominate your life more than God—such as your marriage or your family. Your "god" is whatever you allow to control you, to be the ultimate guide to decision making, the place of your supreme loyalty, and the source of your self-worth.

THE MEANING OF PUTTING GOD FIRST

Imagine your life priorities in terms of a ladder. There is a whole series of levels in terms of what you value. Right now, something is at the top of your list—you really do have a god that you have placed first and foremost above all other things.

Your God

The Bible says that, in order to experience an authentic life of obedience to God, your top priority must be God—the one and only God. But what does that actually mean? Let's play it out.

First, it means you have nothing else *before* God. He really is on top, the first in line. There are no other gods you have allowed into your life or that you have created to challenge God's position at the top of the ladder. You haven't placed God second, third, or anywhere else down the line. There is one and only one place in your life for God—*first*—and that is where you have Him in your life.

One day a campus minister engaged a particular student about the claims of Christ. The student was intellectually intrigued, and after going home and exploring the Bible, he came back the next day and said that he was convinced.

"Great!" the minister replied. "So are you now open to Christ having a place in your life?"

"No," the student replied. "I have a very active sex life. I know Christ would want to change that. I don't want anyone to change that."[2] Even at the earliest stages in his spiritual exploration, the young student knew that an authentic relationship with God would demand putting Him first.

Many of you have already made the commitment to let Christ have control of your life. As a Christian, you have the privilege of an authentic relationship with God because you have come to Him through Jesus Christ, His Son, trusting Him as your Savior and Lord.

But that's not all. Putting God first means having nothing else *besides* God in control of our lives. Some put God at the top of their list—but with a twist: "God *and* . . ."

God *and*

Ever played the "God *and* . . ." game? It's easy to play. All you have to do is want God *and* other things to be first. So you go for God *and* money or God *and* career. You wouldn't dream of saying that God isn't first in your life, but you can't bring yourself to let Him be the only driving force of your life. So you play the "God *and* . . ." game, putting other things in first place alongside Him.³

But that's not what putting God first means. When God commanded us to have no other gods before Him, He meant for us to have no other gods *before* Him, *alongside* of Him, or in *addition* to Him. That's what "no other" means—*no other!* There can only be *one thing* first in your life. God says it must be Him.

BUT WHY?

The first commandment is not particularly complicated. But you may be wondering why putting God first in your life is such a big deal. Is it because God is some kind of insecure, neurotic, easily threatened, egotistical deity who can't handle competition? Is it because God is the cosmic kill-joy, getting bent out of shape if we start enjoying anything else too much?

4

No.

It's because God knows that the only way you will ever experience a fulfilled life is to put Him first. When God—and God alone—is at the top of your list, you will enjoy a sense of peace and security that you have never known. You will panic less. You will love more. You will see your circumstances from God's perspective. You will be able to experience the life of fullness and joy that God always intended for you to live.

But more than that, God also knows that whatever other god you put first in your life will not come through for you when you need it most desperately. At some point, you're going to have trouble. You will experience a need, a crisis, or a tragedy. One day, you will be on the phone dialing a 911 prayer so fast your fingers will burn. Sooner or later, we all experience those moments when it feels as if the wheels are coming off.

It may be happening now.

If you look to something for help that can't come through for you—if you have ordered your life around something other than God—then when your life comes crashing down, no help will come. No cavalry will arrive. You'll be dialing 911, but no one will ever pick up.[4]

Psalm 115 reveals the impotency of false gods: "Our God is in heaven. . . . Their idols are made of silver and gold, the work of human hands. They have mouths, but they cannot speak. They have eyes, but they cannot see. They have ears, but they cannot hear. They have noses, but they cannot smell. They have hands, but they cannot feel. They have feet, but they cannot walk. No sounds come from their throats. People who make idols will be like them, and so will those who trust them" (vv. 3–8 NCV).

Imagine that someone asked you to do the following: "Choose one thing that will be the most important thing in the world to you. You will order your life around it. You will depend on it for everything that matters to you. You will turn to it in times of tragedy and go to it when you need answers to life's most difficult questions. And when you die, you will stake your entire eternity on it."

Then comes the question: "What will it be?"

What would your response be? I can't imagine anyone saying, "Oh, that's easy: my job." Or, "My wife." Or even, "The balance in my checkbook." I think most people would say, "Boy, that one thing better be something a little more reliable, something a little bit bigger." When we really stop and think about it, the first priority in our lives is clear—it's God! But we *don't* stop and think about it. Instead, we put our relationships, our career, our money—you fill in the blank—*first* in our lives! Then we build our lives around it, only to find that it will not come through for us when we need it most. Time and again, we place things of secondary importance in a primary position, ignoring the potential ramifications.

I was preparing to board an airplane from Charlotte to Los Angeles when I noticed a guy who was also waiting to board the plane. I noticed him because he was acting a bit strange— nervous, agitated. You see all types at the airport, so I didn't think too much of it.

When I boarded the plane, nothing happened. And I mean *nothing*. The plane did not prepare to taxi out to the runway. Then

I noticed activity near the front of the plane. Very official-looking people began coming on board, interrogating some of the passengers. I didn't know what was going on until the captain got on the intercom system and said that one of the passengers had bought a one-way ticket to Los Angeles and then boarded with a paper bag. At the last minute, he got off the plane—but without the bag. It was the strange-acting man.

And now, *no one could find the bag*.

As a result, they needed us—as a safety precaution—to get off the plane so that they could check it over. And they checked every inch of that plane. They went through the cabins, the luggage compartments, and the stowaway sections, and they even brought on a bomb-sniffing dog. We had to wait for nearly an hour and a half, but they wanted to make sure everything was secure.

Meanwhile, in the airport, my fellow delayed passengers were griping, complaining, bad-mouthing the airline, and saying that they better get free champagne on the flight to L.A. One woman was reading an attendant the riot act about how late she was going to be. I wanted to go up to her and say, "Lady, if they don't check this plane, you may have a whole new understanding of *late!*"

I was shocked at people's attitudes. It was so bad, I went up to one gal who had taken more than her fair share of negative comments and said, "Listen, I'm glad you're checking this plane this carefully. Take as much time as you need." As it turned out, they didn't find anything. I had a few minutes to talk with the police officer who brought on the bomb-sniffing dog. He said incidents like this happen about two hundred times a year in Charlotte

alone, and they check out every one. The consequences of not putting safety first are too horrible to even think about.

It's no different with God. The consequences of not putting
God first are too horrible to think about as well. As a pastor, it's
an occupational hazard to see this played out, firsthand, time
and time again. Marriages, families, relationships, health, emo-
tions, and careers are devastated and often destroyed as a result
of putting something other than God first. And then, when they
need the thing they have put first to come through for them, it
does not deliver.

That's why this commandment is at the top of God's list. It's the
foundation for an authentic life of obedience to God. God loves
you so much, He wants to make sure you build your life around
Him so that you have the one, true, and only God there to help
you, guide you, and provide for you as you go through life.

Robert Boyd Munger wrote a little book that came out many
years ago called *My Heart, Christ's Home.* In that book, a man
describes what it's like to have Christ come into his heart in terms
of inviting Him into his home.

In the beginning, Jesus came into a house of darkness, turned on
the light, and built a fire in the fireplace to begin driving out the
cold. He then played music where there had been stillness and
brought companionship where there had been loneliness. But that
was only the man's first step in making his heart Christ's home.
Then came the process of having Christ settle down and *be* at
home, as the man showed Him every nook and cranny, corner, and
crevice of his house. Jesus toured the library, which represented the

man's mind; the dining room, which was the room of his appetites and desires; the den, the basement workshop, and the playroom. Finally, Jesus asked about the hall closet.

The man didn't want Jesus to go there. In the closet, behind lock and key, he had hidden things that he didn't want anyone to know and certainly didn't want Christ to see. Then the man realizes what he needs most isn't to keep Christ out, but to have Christ in—and in *everything*.[5]

How to Put God First

So if we want to experience an authentic Christ-life, we have to put God first. But how can we move beyond merely wanting to put God first to making that a reality in our lives? The Bible points to some concrete suggestions to putting this command into practice.

First, if you are not already in a relationship with God by coming to Him through His Son, Jesus Christ, begin that relationship today by saying, "God, I don't deserve to have You come through for me, because I have not come through for You. I have lied, cheated, stolen, and been sexually impure in my thoughts and deeds. . . . I'm sorry, and I ask for Your forgiveness. I want to get right with You."

When you do that, God says, *Deal! Consider it done—I'd love to do that! On the basis of what My Son, Jesus Christ, did on the cross, I forgive you, and we can enter into a relationship.*

If you want to put God first in your life, there is no other beginning. This is first base.

Once you've come to God as your Forgiver and have entered into that relationship, putting Him first means that you then let Him *lead*. Own up to how you *have* been ordering your life, and ask God to forgive you for not putting Him first. This is the second step. There's no such thing as putting God first and not following His lead.

Let's look at this a little closer. The Bible says to stop lying. Some of you have been lying, and you're covering up. God says, "Speak the truth." Your first instinct will be to say, "Wait a minute; I know where I'm lying and why. If I start speaking the truth in those areas, it could get messy!"

Yes, it could. But God has called you to tell the truth.

The Bible talks about honoring God with our bodies. Some of you are sinning sexually. You know it. Your first reaction might be, "But that would mean somebody would have to move out!" Yes, it does. But God has called you to be sexually pure.[6]

"Okay," you say, "let me get this straight. You're telling me that if I want to put God first, I'm actually going to have to *put Him first?* In everything?"

Yes.

Put God first in your finances, your career, your family, your relationships, your sex life, and your time. God's call is for you to be wholly devoted to Him. You may have been dodging that call your whole life. You know that God should be first in your life, but you have never crossed the line. You have never really surrendered to His leadership in every area of your life. Don't wait for your world to come crashing down around you to make you realize that what you've built your life around—what you *have* been putting first—won't come through for you. Because no matter how scared you might be at the prospect of it, no matter how messy following God's lead might seem, no matter how much sacrifice and risk might be involved in putting Him first, don't be a fool.

The stakes are too high.

To live an authentic life, you must answer the call to follow God by putting Him first above everything else, having no other gods before Him. Now here's the challenge—how will you respond?

If you want to put God first in your life, here's a simple prayer that you can pray. Just use it as an outline, a guide, adapting it to your own words and feelings.

Dear God, I am so sorry that I have not put You first in my life. I have put other things before You or alongside You, and I'm sorry. I ask for Your forgiveness through the shed blood of Christ on the cross. Now I want to be an authentic Christian by putting You first in my life. I will take those risks of obedience, finding out what You want and then doing it. I'm scared, but I know that the Holy Spirit will work in my life, and I know that You will be there for me every step of the way. You have said, "Come, follow Me." And for the sake of that call, I'm coming. I'm putting You first.

CHAPTER 2

Making Sure It's God

A former chaplain at Harvard recalls that students would often come into his office and declare, "I don't believe in God." The wise chaplain would then reply, "Sit down and tell me what kind of God you don't believe in. I probably don't believe in that God either."[1]

Like those students, most of us have created a mental picture of God, based on countless feelings, ideas, and past experiences from our life. But do we have a true picture of God?

If we're going to live an authentic life and put God first, we have to make sure that who we're putting first is really God. This is the essence of the second of the Ten Commandments. God said, "You shall not make for yourself an idol in the form of anything in heaven above or on the earth beneath or in the waters below. You shall not bow down to them or worship them" (Exod. 20:4–5).

An idol is something that represents a picture of God, attempting to capture God's essence or image. God instructs us not to create any kind of image that is going to reduce Him to something less than He really is or something that distorts who He really is. Why? Because nothing we could ever make or imagine could begin to accurately reflect God's wonder, power, majesty, and mystery.[2]

By creating a physical image of God, we would place Him in a box, making Him into something smaller and less meaningful than He really is. God would be so distorted that we would end up with a picture of Him that has very little to do with His real character and personality. J. I. Packer has noted that images dishonor God because they obscure His glory, for they are an attempt to create something that reflects the Creator. A false image of God results in a false relationship with a false god.[3]

WHAT DOES THIS HAVE TO DO WITH ME?

Now you're probably saying to yourself, *What in the world does this have to do with me? I haven't made any idols. I haven't bowed down to any statues. Why waste time on this commandment?* Fair question. And my answer might surprise you. I believe that more people— including Christians—are committing idolatry today than at any other time in all of human history. It's one of the greatest areas of disobedience in action today.

Here's why.

The gist of the second commandment is that we should not create an image of God that is not God and then set up that false image *as* God. So *any* image of God—physical *or* mental—that is *less* than who He really is, *misleading* about who He really is, or *replaces* who He really is, is idolatry. Yet today, one of the foundational values of our modern world is that whatever you want to believe about God is okay. Any image, any idea, any concept of God is perfectly acceptable.

An interesting example of our culture's view of God is reflected in *How Do You Spell God?* a book written by a Jewish rabbi and a Catholic priest, with a foreword by the Dalai Lama. It's hard to get much more politically correct than that. The compilation attempts to present an overview of the world's religions and was eventually made into an HBO prime-time special. In the book, the authors describe God in terms of climbing a mountain, noting that everybody knows that there is not just one way to climb a mountain. Mountains are too big for that. They then apply that idea to God, saying that He, too, is too large for one idea or understanding. Therefore all of the ideas about God throughout all of the religions of the world are like different ways up the same mountain. So how do you spell God? Their answer: *Any way you want.* It doesn't matter.

But it does matter.

God is very particular about how we think about Him, picture Him, and define Him. The second commandment says that if we have created anything—whether by our hands *or* through our minds—that is not an accurate picture of God's nature, character, or personality, we have entered into idolatry and left the path of an authentic life.

God is real and alive, and He knows exactly who He is. He wants us to know who He is too, because the only way we can be

15

in an authentic relationship with Him is to know Him authentically. So don't make any physical images that reduce Him to something less than He really is, and don't embrace any mental or philosophical images that misrepresent who He really is. The danger of creating false images of God is that they often lead to the creation of a "folk theology" that simplistically embraces cultural ideas or an informal tradition of beliefs and practices composed mainly of clichés and legends.[4] We would then be tempted to take that image and make it our object of worship, which would mislead us about who He is, create misunderstandings about who He is, and then become a substitute for who He is.

So what kind of false images do we have about God? Not many of us make statues of God and bow down to them, but we may have inaccurate pictures of God in our heads. Here are four common distortions that go against the picture of God as revealed in the Bible.[5]

THE CELESTIAL SANTA CLAUS

The first and perhaps the most common distortion is the picture of God as something like a celestial Santa Claus, a grandfatherly type who smiles at everything we do and then pats us on the head while giving us whatever we want. This is an image of God that is safe, comfortable, convenient, warm, and fuzzy—regardless of how we live. Because even though we are *told* that Santa Claus knows who has been naughty or nice and that there are stockings filled with coal for bad little boys and girls, the Christmas presents always seem to come. Santa is simply too nice and jolly to do anything else!

According to the Bible, this picture of God is not accurate. Sometimes Christians even try to make God into a benign, jolly gift giver by focusing on His forgiveness and grace to the exclusion of His holiness and justice. We may *want* God to be like jolly ol' Saint Nicholas so that we can live however we want without having to deal with the implications of His holiness, but that's not who the Bible says God really is. The Bible presents a God who is to be taken very, very seriously.

The prophet Isaiah was one of the holiest men of his generation. He was the spiritual leader of his day, and he had an authentic relationship with God. The Bible records that Isaiah once actually encountered the living God. It is interesting to notice how this holy man in a good relationship with God responded to the actual *presence* of God:

> In the year that King Uzziah died, I saw the Lord seated on a throne, high and exalted, and the train of his robe filled the temple. Above him were seraphs, each with six wings: With two wings they covered their faces, with two they covered their feet, and with two they were flying. And they were calling to one another:
>
> "Holy, holy, holy is the LORD Almighty; the whole earth is full of his glory."
>
> At the sound of their voices the doorposts and thresholds shook and the temple was filled with smoke.

"Woe to me!" I cried. "I am ruined! For I am a man of unclean lips, and I live among a people of unclean lips, and my eyes have seen the King, the LORD Almighty." (Isa. 6:1–5)

That's not a response you'd give to a harmless, grandfatherly, Santa Claus—but it is the response you would give to the sovereign and holy God of the universe.

THE BIG MAN

Some of the false pictures of God running around the Christian landscape that can be falsely worshiped have less to do with His character than His nature. One of the most common is to see God as little more than a "big man," sort of a John Wayne figure that is very much like us, only more. Christians who perceive God as a humanlike deity often glibly refer to Him as the "man upstairs" or the "big guy." Movies have taken this image of God and cemented it into our minds through the *Oh, God* movies with George Burns and, in a more subtle fashion, through the humanistic treatment of angels portrayed by John Travolta in *Michael* or Nicolas Cage in *City of Angels*.

But God is *not* a human being. He is not even an *advanced* human being. He is a Person, and He is personal, but that is where the comparison ends. Instead, the Bible says that "God is spirit" (John 4:24), and He is "the King eternal, immortal, invisible, the only God" (1 Tim. 1:17). While the Bible often uses physical imagery as a literary device to discuss the personality of God, God is not made of flesh and blood. His nature and being go far beyond an advanced, superhuman version of ourselves. "God is not the sort of person we are," writes J. I. Packer. "His wisdom, His aims, His scale of values, His mode of procedure differ so vastly from our own that we cannot possibly guess our way to them by intuition or infer them by analogy from our notion of ideal manhood."[6]

THE FORCE

Yet if there are some images of God that are too human, some are not human enough! One of the latest spiritual trends is to try alternative brands of spirituality, as evidenced by the growing number of Hollywood movie stars dabbling in Buddhism or New Age thought. These other spiritualities teach that the whole universe is divine and we are part of that divine oneness.

The *Star Wars* movies are good examples of the overwhelming popularity of the idea that God is a divine, impersonal oneness. In 1997, the initial trilogy opened to packed houses twenty years after their initial debut. During the summer of 1999, a new installment initiating a second trilogy was released to record box-office receipts, second only to *Titanic* for the entire decade. In the first movie, which was Episode IV in George Lucas's mind, Luke Skywalker meets an old man named Obi-Wan Kenobi, who was a Jedi Knight. Obi-Wan gives Luke his father's light saber and instructs him on the ways of the "Force." He tells young Luke that the Force is what gives the Jedi his power. It's an energy field created by all living things. It surrounds us and penetrates us, binding the galaxy together. Obi-wan also tells Luke that there is a dark side of the Force and a good side of the Force, and that he should beware the dark side.

Christians can sometimes get caught up in the idea that God is some kind of impersonal, pervading force present in everything. But the Bible clearly shows us that this is a misrepresentation of the true nature and identity of God. Although the Bible does teach that God is Spirit, that He surrounds and guides the universe, and that He is present everywhere, everything is *not* God. You and I are not *part* of God; we are created *by* God in the image of God. Notice how the Bible talks about the creation of the world and human beings: "In the beginning God created the heavens and the earth. . . . God created man in his own image, in the image of God he created him; male and female he created them" (Gen. 1:1, 27).

We are distinct from God, yet we are personal beings. We have that personality because we were made in the image of God and God is personal. This is the very basis of Christianity: God is Person, and He wants to be in a personal relationship with each and every one of us.

Rather than an impersonal "force," think of a Father.

Philip Yancey writes about a friend of his who was in conflict with his fifteen-year-old daughter. He knew she was using birth control, and several nights she had not bothered to come home at all. As parents, he and his wife had tried various forms of punishment, but nothing seemed to make much of a difference. Their daughter lied to them, deceived them, and always found a way to turn the tables on them, blaming her behavior on her parents for being so strict.

Yancey's friend said that he remembered standing before the plate-glass window in his living room one night, staring out into the darkness, waiting for his daughter to come home. He said he felt such rage. He wanted to be like the father in the parable of the prodigal son, but he was furious with his daughter for the way she would manipulate him and his wife and intentionally hurt them. And, of course, she was hurting herself more than anyone. He said that he began to understand the passages in the Bible expressing God's frustration—passages that talked about how the people knew how to wound God and how God would cry out in pain.

"But then," he said, "when my daughter came home that night, or rather the next morning, I wanted nothing in the world so much as to take her in my arms, to love her, to tell her I wanted the best for her. I was a lovesick father."

Yancey writes that now, when he thinks about God, he holds up that image—the image of the lovesick father. Because as he has reflected on it, it's the most biblical image you could have. Not an impersonal force, but a God who is standing in front of the plate-glass window gazing achingly into the darkness, waiting for His child to come home.[7]

THE SPECIAL FEELING

One final distortion of God creeping into the Christian church is to reduce God to little more than a feeling and then worshiping the feeling. This can be a sense of the sacred through reserved ritual as quickly as it can be a quest for the euphoric through unrestrained enthusiasm. Rather than worshiping the God of the universe, we seek a feeling, a mood, or an emotional experience that we, in turn, worship as if it were God. It's not that we intend to do this, any more than we intend to reduce God to a Santa Claus figure, a big man, or an impersonal force. But if we are not careful, God is not Someone outside of us, but something within us—a part of our inner world that we seek to have touched and energized and brought to the surface through our senses. And it's the sense we seek, the feeling we lift up, rather than God Himself.

FINDING THE RIGHT PICTURE

So where do you get the right picture of God? If you don't want false images floating around in your head, much less your heart, where do you get the real thing? The Bible gives a clear and specific answer: The fullest, most accurate picture of God is found in Jesus Christ—and nowhere else.

The best way for God to reveal Himself to humans was to become a human. Jesus was God in human form. In Colossians, the Bible says, "For in Christ all the fullness of the Deity lives in bodily form" (2:9). And in Hebrews, the Bible teaches, "The Son is the radiance of God's glory and the exact representation of his being" (1:3). Christ is the only accurate and complete picture of the character, attributes, and personality of God. God didn't want us to be confused or misled, so in Jesus He gave us the full picture, the accurate picture—the *only* picture of Himself.

Every January, we celebrate a special Sunday—Super Bowl Sunday. Millions of people tune in to watch the game, so advertisers work overtime to prepare thirty-second spots, each designed for a single purpose: to convey a particular image of their company's product. Portraying this image is so crucial that they will spend millions in production costs and then tens of thousands of dollars per second to air their commercial during the game—all to get across an image. These advertisers know that the right image is important.

God knows it too.

God didn't reveal Himself in a thirty-second advertising spot; He revealed Himself through the thirty-three-year life of Jesus Christ. If you want to know God as He really is, take a long, hard look at Jesus' life and character. Jesus Himself said, "Anyone who has seen me has seen the Father" (John 14:9).

Knowing the picture of God revealed in Jesus and putting your trust in Him are critical, because an accurate understanding of God is the essence of our faith. We are real people with real problems and real issues. We need God as He *really* is—not a false god, not something we've created with our hands or made up in our minds, but the real thing.[8] God is not a character from a work of fiction, and He is not a literary device. He is the Being who holds the cosmos together with a mere thought. Moving from the idea of God, through the false ideas of God, to the real God, is the foundation of an authentic spiritual life.

On the wall above where I am writing is an enlarged photograph of Addison's Walk in Oxford, England. I took the picture on my first trip there and look at it often, for it holds deep meaning for me. On Saturday, September 19, 1931, C. S. Lewis invited two friends to dine with him in his rooms at Magdalen College of Oxford. One was a man by the name of Hugo Dyson, a lecturer in English literature at Reading University. The other guest was none other than the famed author of *The Hobbit* and *The Lord of the Rings*, J. R. R. Tolkien.

On that fall evening, after they had dined, Lewis took his guests on a walk through the Magdalen grounds, ending with a stroll down Addison's Walk, a path that runs beside several streams of the River Cherwell, with an entrance just beside the building in which Lewis resided. It was there they began to discuss the idea of metaphor and myth.

Lewis had long appreciated myths. As a boy, he had loved the great Norse stories of the dying god Balder, and as a man, he grew to love and appreciate the power of myths throughout the history of language and literature. But he didn't *believe* in them. Beautiful and moving though they might be, he concluded that they were ultimately untrue. As he expressed to Tolkien, myths are "lies and therefore worthless, even though breathed through silver."

"No," insisted Tolkien. "They are not lies."

Later, Lewis recalled that at the moment Tolkien uttered those words, "a rush of wind . . . came so suddenly on the still, warm evening and sent so many leaves pattering down that we thought it was raining. We held our breath." Tolkien's point was that the great myths were not all just lies, but they might just reflect a splintered fragment of the true light. Within the myth was something of eternal truth. They talked on, and Lewis became convinced by the force of Tolkien's argument.

They returned to Lewis's rooms. Once there, they turned their conversation to Christianity. Here, Tolkien argued, the poet who invented the story was none other than God Himself, and the images He used were real men and women in actual history.

Lewis was floored. "Do you mean," he asked, "that the death and resurrection of Christ is the old 'dying God' story all over again?"

"Yes," Tolkien answered, "except that here is a *real* dying God, with a precise location in history and definite historical consequences. The old myth has become fact."

It was now 3 A.M., and Tolkien had to go home. Lewis and Dyson escorted him down the stairs. They crossed the quadrangle and let him out by the little postern gate on Magdalen Bridge. Lewis later recalled, "Dyson and I found more to say to one another, strolling up and down the cloister of New Building, so that we did not get to bed till 4."

Twelve days later, Lewis wrote to his close friend from boyhood, Arthur Greeves: "I have just passed on from believing in God to definitely believing in Christ—in Christianity. I will try to explain this another time. My long night talk with Dyson and Tolkien had a good deal to do with it."[9]

Lewis had moved beyond the myth to fact—to the reality of God as He really is—and, like many others who have discovered the true image of God, it transformed his life.

CHAPTER 3

Taking God Seriously

How do you know when to take someone seriously? For many, it starts with his or her name. I know it did with my parents and me. I was born with the given name of James Emery White. My grandfather's name was Henry James White, and my great-grandfather's name was Robert Emery Thompson. So the names "James" and "Emery" were unique to my heritage.

Today, friends call me "Jim." But that was not what I was called at birth. I was called "Emery." And not just at birth, but on every day, by every single person in my life, for the first six years of my life. That was my name: *Emery* White. From birth, my parents chose to call me by my middle name. It was the only name I went by and the only name that entered my parents' minds when they thought of their son.

But on the first day of kindergarten, when everybody was learning everybody else's name, one of the children made a mistake with mine. Instead of calling me Emery, he called me "Ann

Marie." I was none too pleased. Hell hath no fury like a six-year-old whose name is mispronounced on the first day of kindergarten, much less when that six-year-old victim is a boy and the mispronunciation is the name of a *girl!* Even at six, I knew what was at stake: My very masculinity was on the line. The next day, I announced to the class that I was no longer Emery, but Jim. My teacher called my mother, thinking she should know. When I came home, I gathered my family around me and declared, "I have decided that I am not going to be called Emery anymore. I want to be called Jim. That is what I want my name to be."

Now you can imagine how that went over with my parents, who had chosen the name Emery and had called me Emery for six years. Yet I stuck to my convictions and seemed to be very sure of what I wanted. And believe it or not, they honored it. I have been "Jim" ever since.

Our names are important to us, aren't they? God's name matters to Him too. In the third commandment, God says: "You shall not misuse the name of the LORD your God, for the LORD will not hold anyone guiltless who misuses his name" (Exod. 20:7).

A name is serious business. It represents who someone is. Whenever you use that name, you bring that person to mind. You make a direct reference to who they are. And the name is either right or wrong. Fair or an injustice. Accurate or misleading. Honoring or a form of ridicule.

Number three on God's top-ten list is a command for us to be careful with God's name. Why? Because we should be cautious with

God. He is not Someone to be toyed with. The third commandment instructs us to take God seriously. We are not to refer to Him in a way that is empty, insincere, or cavalier. This commandment is like a big sign near a power plant that says, "Warning. High Voltage."[1] Robert Webber has interpreted this commandment as "Never live as though God does not exist."[2]

Just think about how it works in other areas of life in which everything hinges on giving something or someone the respect they deserve. If a prizefighter underestimates his opponent, he doesn't prepare like he should, and so he loses. If a student doesn't take a class seriously, when it comes time to take a test, he or she will fail. If a child doesn't learn to respect the power of electricity and sticks a fork into a light socket, that child is in for a shock.

C. R. Smith was one of the founders of American Airlines, and he once made a stopover in Nashville, Tennessee. When he did, he found two desks in the American Airlines corridor of the airport. On one, a phone was ringing away. Sitting at the other, with his feet propped up, was a man reading a newspaper.

Smith walked up to him and said, "Your phone is ringing."

"That's reservations. I'm maintenance," the man replied.

Furious, Smith walked over to the desk, picked up the phone, and began talking to a man who urgently needed to get to California. Smith rattled off the schedule from memory to the man and hung up. The man from maintenance couldn't believe it!

"Say, that was pretty good!" he said. "Do you work for American?"

"Yes, I do," Smith answered. "And you used to."[3]

It's important to learn what to take seriously—and *who.* Nothing should be taken more seriously than God, and giving God His proper respect starts with His name, because His name represents who He is. This is why the Bible says, "Holy and awesome is his name. The fear of the LORD is the beginning of wisdom; all who follow his precepts have good understanding" (Ps. 111:9–10).

Those who have encountered God would concur. Of his pivotal spiritual experience in which he encountered the presence of the living God, French philosopher and mathematician Blaise Pascal was so overwhelmed that he could only write a single word: *fire.*

The Jewish people understood the magnificence of God's name. When God told Moses to go to the highest authority in Egypt and demand the release of all the Hebrew slaves, Moses asked God to give him His name so that he could say to the people exactly who had sent him. The answer God gave to Moses is intriguing: "God said to Moses, 'I AM WHO I AM. This is what you are to say . . . 'I AM has sent me to you'" (Exod. 3:14). That phrase—"I AM"— came to be considered the most holy word in existence to the Jewish people, for it was the very name of God. God's name was so revered that the Jews would not even write it completely out, but they only write the consonants, resulting in YHWH.[4]

Yet a respect for God's name runs deeper than merely watching our words. So how do we maintain that same level of reverence, carrying out the spirit of this command for our life? Let's find the answer by walking through three ways we have a tendency to misuse God's name.

THE MISUSE OF GOD'S NAME
THROUGH PROFANITY

The first misuse of God's name is through profanity. The word *profane* comes from two words: *pro,* which means "out of," and *fanus,* which means "temple." So profanity is using God's name in any way that is outside of its proper spiritual home, or context.[5]

Profanity is a serious breach of conduct and character, for it reveals where we stand in respect to—and in respect of—God. Let's face it; certain statements are dead giveaways about people.[6] If you were to hear someone say, "One of the problems with investing in penny stocks is that the buy/sell spread can be as high as 90 percent," it would be reasonable to assume that you were listening to a financial planner or investment counselor. If you were to overhear that somebody was downloading new executable files and associated DLLs, you could assume that you were listening to a computer programmer. If you were in a hospital and overheard someone say, "She's dilated to eight centimeters and her epidural is in place," you could be reasonably confident that you were overhearing an obstetrician, or perhaps an obstetrics assistant.

What can you tell about someone you hear saying, "Oh God!" or "God damn it!" in a fit of anger? What about an exasperated use of "Jesus Christ" or a bitten-off "Jesus"? You may not be able to draw conclusions about that person's vocation, race, gender, or income, but you can tell a lot about his or her heart, not to mention his or her disposition toward God. In Luke 6:45, Jesus said, "Whatever is in the heart overflows into speech" (TLB). For some,

31

profane language may stem from being uninformed, uncontrolled, or outside of a relationship with God, but the bottom line is that profanity, in any form, is a failure to take God seriously.

THE MISUSE OF GOD'S NAME FOR OUR BENEFIT

A second way that you can misuse God's name is to misuse it for your own benefit. In ancient times, names were considered to be very powerful. Many people thought that if you used someone's name, some of his or her power flowed directly to you. In a way, we still hold to that idea. It's called "name-dropping." We use the name of another person in the belief that it will enhance our reputations or benefit our lives. The hope is that some of that person's power, prestige, or influence will flow to us.

It is possible to do the same thing with God. At the most basic level, we misuse God's name when we try to get someone to believe us by saying, "I swear to God it's true." In His famous Sermon on the Mount, recorded in Matthew 5:34–37, Christ warned us against implicating God's holy name by swearing the truth of something: "Do not swear at all: either by heaven, for it is God's throne; or by the earth, for it is his footstool; or by Jerusalem, for it is the city of the Great King. And do not swear by your head, for you cannot make even one hair white or black. Simply let your 'Yes' be 'Yes,' and your 'No,' 'No'; anything beyond this comes from the evil one."

The misuse of God's name for personal profit is easily applied to certain televangelists who use the name of God to make a buck off of overly trusting people, or politicians who mention God's name in the right places and at the right times in order to gain a certain constituency of voters. It is widely known that former president Richard Nixon courted evangelist Billy Graham's personal friendship for political advantage. When Billy read the Watergate transcripts for the first time, chock-full of Nixon's profanity, manipulation, cover-ups, and power plays, he became so upset that he went into the bathroom and vomited.[7]

But this misuse of God's name also hits closer to home. We use the name of God for our benefit when we claim God's name for our own agenda, our own ambition, and our own gain. Years ago in Germany, there was a young Jewish boy who had a profound sense of admiration for his father. His family's life centered on the acts of piety and devotion prescribed by their religion. The father was zealous in attending worship and religious instruction, and he demanded the same from his children. While the boy was a teenager, the family was forced to move to another town in Germany. There was no synagogue in the new town, and the pillars of the community all belonged to the Lutheran church. Suddenly the father announced to the family that they were going to abandon their Jewish traditions and join the Lutheran church. When the stunned family asked why, the father explained that changing religions was necessary to help his business.

The youngster was bewildered and confused. His deep disappointment soon gave way to anger and a kind of intense bitterness that plagued him throughout his life. That disappointed son, disillusioned by his father's lack of integrity, eventually left

Germany and went to England to study. He sat daily at the British Museum, formulating various ideas and writing a book. In that work, he introduced an entirely new world-view, envisioning a movement that would change the social and political systems of the world. Drawing from past experiences with his father, he described religion as an "opiate for the masses" that could be explained totally in terms of economics and personal gain. Today, millions of people still live under the system invented by this embittered man, and millions more suffered under previous regimes that incorporated its values. His name, of course, was Karl Marx, and his idea was communism. And it all began with his father's misuse of the name of God for the sake of profit.[8]

But violating this command doesn't have to involve things as crass as the pursuit of financial gain. It can be much more subtle, involving the use of God's name for personal fulfillment or recognition—something we humans are all too tempted to pursue. In 1997, the *New York Times* reported that, during the construction of a six-million-dollar children's zoo in New York's Central Park, a couple who had agreed to donate half the money to the project was withdrawing their three-million-dollar contribution. The problem was that they didn't like where the plaque that would acknowledge their gift was going to be placed. It wasn't going to be large enough or central enough to their liking. In the place of their liking was a plaque in honor of the founders of the zoo, lovingly positioned thirty-six years earlier. The couple wanted that plaque taken down and one for them put up in its place. The commission refused, so they took back their gift. When interviewed, the fickle donors said that they were not asking for neon lights, just the "proper acknowledgment for a sizeable gift."[9] Our hunger for recognition and honor can tempt us to take the most noble of acts and turn them into self-serving pursuits.

To honor God's name is to give Him the honor instead of using it for our own benefit. While in London one summer, I visited St. Paul's cathedral, often cited as perhaps the most powerful architectural statement ever made in the old city. St. Paul's was designed and built by the famed architect Christopher Wren. Begun in 1675, the cathedral took thirty-five years to build. As I wandered inside, amazed at its beauty and detail, grace and precision, I noticed there was nothing inside commemorating Wren himself. This struck me as strange, since St. Paul's housed more than three hundred monuments to others. As I stood in the middle of the cathedral, gazing around, I happened to look down and see a small, circular marker signifying that someone was buried underneath.

It was the tomb of Christopher Wren.

I learned later that Wren didn't want a monument to himself at all, wishing instead for all honor to flow to God. Yet those who knew him and marveled at his work couldn't resist. Keeping with the spirit of his request, they placed the marker on the floor, with the following words in Latin circling its borders: "Beneath lies buried the founder of this church and city Christopher Wren, who lived more than ninety years not for himself but for the public good. Reader, if you seek his monument, look around you." Or as Wren himself might have added, "Look above you."

YOU CAN EXPERIENCE . . . AN AUTHENTIC LIFE

The Misuse of God's Name by Pretending

The third way to misuse God's name is the most offensive of all, which is to misuse it through pretending. This is when we use His name as if we are in a relationship with Him, but in reality, we do not know Him personally. We say we believe in God, but our lives don't reflect it. We use God's name, but we are not God's people.

A soldier who fought under Alexander the Great apparently hadn't fleshed out the kind of character and courage and commitment that the great leader expected from his followers. Alexander called the man to appear in front of him. The soldier stood before his commander—poorly dressed, slouching, and completely out of sync with what was expected of those in the legendary army that conquered much of the known world of its day.

"What is your name?" demanded Alexander.

"My name is Alexander. The same as yours," answered the man.

"Change your name," returned Alexander the Great, "or change your ways."[10]

Jesus felt the same way about people who claimed His name without supporting it with a holy life, once asking, "Why do you keep on saying that I am your Lord, when you refuse to do what I say?" (Luke 6:46 CEV). The word *Christian* literally means "little Christ." It was first ascribed to the band of Christ-followers in Antioch as a term that others felt best reflected who they were and how they lived. They were like "little Christs." Yet many who call themselves Christians today reflect little of Christ.

When I was a freshman in college, I had a roommate named

Adam, who was a Mormon. I was a bizarre combination of things at that stage in my life. I was well read in Christian works, versed in theology, solid in world-view, and carnal to my core in lifestyle and disposition. At the age of eighteen, I could quote C. S. Lewis and Francis Schaeffer, discuss the finer points of a freewill theodicy, and top it off with an all-night party that threw abandon to the wind. And that's putting it mildly.

Not long into our new rooming situation, Adam and I talked about religion. Using the latest apologetics maneuverings, I proceeded to dismantle my friend's spiritual moorings. He had few answers, and I was enjoying myself immensely. Suddenly, with disarming accuracy, Adam launched a counteroffensive that pinpointed the fundamental weakness in my argument and left me without any hope of reply.

"Jim, how can you stand there and tell me anything about my life with the way you live?"

That single sentence placed me on the road to salvation. It revealed my faith for what it was—a mockery of the very name of God. I called myself a Christian, and I certainly believed in the Christian faith, but I carried the name without respect, honor, or meaning.

When we misuse God's name through profanity, selfish gain, or as false advertising in regard to who we really are—we trivialize God. We make Him insignificant, meaningless, and marginal. Soon, we do not take God seriously at all.

Until the end.

Then, no matter how you've treated God's name, you'll take it very seriously. The Bible says that "man is destined to die once, and after that to face judgment" (Heb. 9:27). On Judgment Day, you will stand before a holy God, and your life—all of your choices, decisions, actions, and attitudes—will be revealed for what they really were. And this judgment is for everyone. All human beings will stand before God and answer for their lives. I will, and you will. The Bible says, "We will all stand before God's judgment seat. . . . Each of us will give an account of himself to God" (Rom. 14:10, 12). I will answer for how I've used God's name. At that moment, His name will mean everything to me. How I treated, spoke, used, and reflected on God's name will become the most serious thing in the world.

A Word to Our Children

A few years ago, my wife and I were getting ready to take our very first overseas trip together. I don't know whether it was flying on the plane together for such a long time, being gone for nearly two weeks, or going halfway around the world from our kids, but we started to get paranoid about what would happen if *something* happened. So we started double-checking our life insurance and making sure that guardian and custody issues were settled with family members in the case of our death. We even considered taking separate flights so that if one crashed, our kids would still have one parent.

Yet after all of the safety issues and financial issues and legal issues were settled, we were still left with the *emotional* issue, because all of the lawyers and wills and insurance agents had made us emotional *wrecks*. So we ended up doing one more thing before we left. We sat down and wrote a letter to our kids that we gave to our parents—to be given to our children in the case of our death. It was the hardest, most emotional letter I've ever written. It wasn't very long. But as Susan worked with me in writing it, it became very clear what mattered most to us in regard to our four young, precious children. Let me share part of it with you:

Dear children:

For reasons we will never understand on this earth, God has decided to take your mommy and daddy home with Him. We are very sorry for the sadness this will bring to you. Remember that as Christians, we never really say good-bye. One day we will see you in heaven, and there will be no more tears.

Of all the things that we tried to give you, nothing was more important than our faith in Christ as Savior and Lord. Never turn away from God. Walk with Him throughout your life. Nothing is more important than this. Up to this moment, all of you have turned your hearts to Him, and we have been so proud.

To Rebecca, our princess, and Rachel, our sunshine: We couldn't have two more beautiful daughters. As you grow, guard your lives. If you marry, give your husband the gift of purity that God intended for marriage, and please, be sure that he knows Christ intimately. Your father has tried to model for you what to look for in a man—do not accept less. Both of you can do anything you want to with your life— you have the intellect, personality, gifts, and talents. Don't let anyone ever tell you differently!

To Jonathan, our best buddy, and Zachary, our squirtster and little man: What parents could have two sons they could be prouder of! As you grow into maturity, remember the model your mother gave you of a woman who was beautiful on the outside and the inside. If you marry, be sure she's someone who loves Christ with all of her heart. Give your lives to God, and remember—you can do anything you want, for you are remarkable young men with more potential than any young men we know. And the world needs men who will make history for the cause of Christ— be those men!

We love you all so much and want only that you love God and live lives that make a difference for Christ. And we will be watching from heaven, rooting you on, and looking forward to that day when we can wrap you in our arms and tell you how proud we were of your life.

Love,
Daddy and Mommy

Writing that letter was a defining moment for us as parents and as Christians. When it came down to life and death, our last words and final thoughts, what mattered most to us in terms of our children was that they take God seriously. We saw with crystal clarity that the most important issue for their lives was where they stood in relation to the name of God.

And isn't that true for all of us?

CHAPTER 4

Calling for Time

I read of a hard-hat employee who filled out a company accident form about what had happened when he had tried to do some repair work following the impact of a storm:

> When I got to the building, I found that the hurricane had knocked off some bricks around the top. So I rigged up a beam with a pulley at the top of the building and hoisted up a couple barrels full of bricks. When I had fixed the damaged area, there were a lot of bricks left over. Then I went to the bottom and began releasing the line. Unfortunately, the barrel of bricks was much heavier than I was—and before I knew what was happening the barrel started coming down, jerking me up.
>
> I decided to hang on since I was too far off the ground by then to jump, and halfway up I met the barrel of bricks coming down fast. I received a hard blow on my shoulder.

I then continued to the top, banging my head against the beam and getting my fingers pinched and jammed in the pulley. When the barrel hit the ground hard, it burst its bottom, allowing the bricks to spill out. I was now heavier than the barrel. So I started down again at high speed. Halfway down I met the barrel coming up fast and received severe injuries to my shins.

When I hit the ground, I landed on the pile of spilled bricks, getting several painful cuts and deep bruises. At this point I must have lost my presence of mind, because I let go of my grip on the line. The barrel came down fast—giving me another blow on my head and putting me in the hospital.

I respectfully request sick leave.[1]

I hope he got it. We all need breaks and rest, vacations and sabbaticals—not just when the bricks of the world fall on our heads, but in order to follow the rhythm and pace of life that God intended.

This is the essence of the fourth of the Ten Commandments. Calling for time. God says, "Remember the Sabbath day by keeping it holy. Six days you shall labor and do all your work, but the seventh day is a Sabbath to the LORD your God. On it you shall not do any work" (Exod. 20:8–10).

But many see this command as anything but restful.

Laura Ingalls Wilder captured the spirit and soul of the early pioneers of the American West in a series of books that have become cherished by young and old alike. In *Little House in the Big*

Woods, she writes that on Sundays, she and her sister Mary could not run or shout or be noisy in their play:

> Mary could not sew on her nine-patch quilt, and Laura could not knit on the tiny mittens she was making for Baby Carrie. They might look quietly at their paper dolls, but they must not make anything new for them. They were not allowed to sew on doll clothes, not even with pins. They must sit quietly and listen while Ma read Bible stories to them. . . . They might look at pictures, and they might hold their rag dolls nicely and talk to them. But there was nothing else they could do.

One Sunday after supper, Laura could not bear it any longer. She began to play with her dog, Jack, and in a few minutes she was running and shouting. Her father told her to sit in her chair and be quiet, but when Laura sat down she began to cry and kick the chair with her heels. "I hate Sunday!" she said.[2]

Almanzo, her future husband, shared her feelings. In *Farmer Boy*, Wilder writes that on Sunday, "Almanzo just sat. He had to. He was not allowed to do anything else, for Sunday was not a day for working or playing. It was a day for going to church and for sitting still." No wonder that by the end of the day, even a nine-year-old boy was "glad when it was time to do the chores."[3]

But that's not the intent of this command. To begin with, the word *Sabbath* does not mean Sunday, or Saturday, or even worship. It literally means to cease, to stop, or to quit. In Genesis, when the Bible describes the creation of the world, we read: "By the seventh day God had finished the work he had been doing; so on the seventh day he rested from all his work. And God blessed the seventh day and made it holy, because on it he rested from all the work of creating that he had done'" (2:2–3).

It's important to note that the best translation of the Hebrew word is actually not "rest," but the cessation of activity related to the work of creation. Emphasizing the English word *rest* has led some people to misinterpret this to mean that on Sundays you aren't supposed to do anything. That's not it at all. The point of the special nature of the seventh day is to have a time of renewal, pleasure, and reflection. The seventh day is a time to cease "doing" and to concentrate on "being."

Let's define some other key words related to God's command. The word *holy* refers to something different, set apart, unique, and unlike anything else. The term *labor* has to do with our regular work and daily duties. And doing something "to the Lord" means that you dedicate it to Him. You give it to Him. So the fourth commandment plays out this way: Every seven days, call for time. And then use that time for a Sabbath.

WHY IS THIS ON GOD'S LIST?

And God put the command for rest on His list for a very important reason: He cares about us. He wants us to live life the way He meant for it to be lived. He knew that if He didn't command us to call for time, we'd forget that there is more to life than work, and we would manage our lives in a destructive way—namely, through workaholism and marginless living.

Workaholism

Most of us are familiar with the term *workaholic*. It was coined by Dr. Wayne Oates in 1968 in an article he wrote for a psychology journal. I had the pleasure of studying under Dr. Oates during part of my graduate-school years. He chose the word *workaholic* because of his observation that work is like a narcotic—it can become compulsive, difficult to handle with restraint and moderation, much like alcoholism or other addictive disorders.

Some of us are *identity* workaholics. Our work defines us, so we build our lives around it. We live for the recognition, the awards, and the prestige. Others of us are *perfectionists*. We put in the long hours because something within us has to make everything perfect. We can't stand anything less than the ideal. Some of us work compulsively for *approval*. We're afraid of saying no to anybody's request for our time and energy. In order to please, we stay late and work through the weekend.

Some of us are *situational* workaholics. We tell ourselves that the long hours are only temporary and will soon pass—but then there's always another big project, another crisis, another season, and it never ends. So every night, the laptop and cell phone come home. Others of us are *escapists*, workaholics because we don't want to have to face what awaits us at home, such as a troubled marriage. Work becomes a haven from the outside world or, more commonly, from our private lives and relationships. Some of us are *materialist* workaholics, who just want more and more and more of what money brings, so we work and work and work to get it.[4] Proverbs 23:4 addresses the materialist workaholic head-on: "Do not wear yourself out to get rich; have the wisdom to show restraint."

But no matter what kind of workaholic you might be, the fourth commandment reveals that there's more to life than work. There's more to *you* than work. There comes a time when enough is enough, and you have to *say* that enough is enough.

Marginless Living

But there's a second reason that God commands us to call for time: If we don't, we put ourselves on a path to self-destruction through marginless living.[5] Dr. Martin Moore-Ede wrote a book called *The Twenty-Four-Hour Society.* He charts how we have developed a society that never sleeps, never quits, and never stops. His conclusion is blunt and to the point: We are not built for the world we have made. Why? Because we have designed a world that ignores the law of limits. It's like a bank account from which we keep making withdrawals but never any deposits.[6]

And he's right. The twenty-four-hour society is what *we* have created. *Time* magazine did an article called "How America Has Run Out of Time," discussing what kids, schedules, jobs, and the modern pace of life have done to our time. It was easy to read the report and say, "Yeah, I knew that was it. It's not my fault; it's just life." But then Robert Samuelson of *Newsweek* magazine did a follow-up piece on the *Time* article that took issue with its premise and offered a telling insight. He said that we just *feel* that life is busier and fuller and more demanding than before, *but it's not.* While time pressures are real—traffic does get congested, and being a working parent is demanding—the facts are that the length of our workday in America is shorter now than ever before, we have more leisure time than ever before, and we own more timesaving devices than ever before. Samuelson concludes with this observation: Time isn't flying—we are.[7]

Even our kids are overscheduled and overworked. Throughout 1997, researchers at the University of Michigan's Institute for Social Research compiled the time diaries of more than thirty-five hundred kids under the age of twelve. On average, kids between the ages of three and twelve spent twenty-nine hours a week in school, which is eight hours more than they did in 1981. They also did more household chores, accompanied their parents on more errands, and participated in more organized activities, like soccer and ballet, than ever before. All in all, children's leisure time—defined as time left over after sleeping, eating, personal hygiene, and attending school or day care—dropped from 40 percent of the day in 1981 to only 25 percent of the day in 1997.

In a magazine article reporting on the study, a profile was given of a young boy named Steven Guzman, who is only twelve but booked solid. He wakes up at 6:00 every weekday morning, downs a five-minute breakfast, reports to school at 7:50, returns home at 3:15, hits the books from 5:00 to 9:00 with a break for dinner, and then goes to bed at 10:30. Saturdays are not much better: From 9:00 to 5:00 he attends a prep program in the hope of getting a scholarship to a private school. Then there are the piano lessons, along with a couple of hours of practice a week. If he's lucky, he'll squeeze in his friends on Sunday. "Sometimes I think, like, since I'm a kid, I need to enjoy my life," young Steven is quoted as saying, "but I don't have time for that."[8]

But we need that kind of time.

Newsweek did a cover story on the president of Harvard University, Neil Rudenstine. The cover showed his picture, underscored by a single word: *Exhausted.* Inside there was a lengthy article titled "Breaking Point," which detailed how this man hit the wall through a life filled with tasks, deadlines, quotas, and engagements. He collapsed under the weight of it all and was forced into a three-month sabbatical by his physician.[9] A second article came out only a few weeks later on how Mike Krzyzewski had left his position as head coach of the Duke basketball team. Though he pointed to a bulging disk in his back, the article was generated by an ESPN interview in which he confessed that it was really more about a "bulging life." He looked around, and the daughter he thought was eight was now twelve. His marriage was suffering. And his life had become saturated with activity to the point that it began to fall apart.[10]

Can you identify with either one of those men?

All of life pushed to the limit. Racing here, pushing it there, extending ourselves somewhere else. We run the race as hard as we can, but then we reach a point at which we just can't run it anymore. We max out, we hit the wall, and we burn out. When we don't take time to rest and turn ourselves toward personal, emotional, and spiritual renewal, then our relationships suffer, we lose perspective on life, we crash and burn emotionally, and we lose touch with God.[11] This is why the fourth commandment tells us to call for time: It is an expression of God's incredible love and concern and compassion for us.

How to Honor a Sabbath

So how do you honor the Sabbath? It's really not complicated, but it does involve four things.

Set Aside the Day

First, you have to set aside the day. You have to set it aside, protect it, and put it on your calendar. Now here's what you'll want to do—at least I know it's what I told *myself* I could do. Rather than a whole day every week, I would tell myself that I was taking little Sabbaths, little rests, little breaks, all throughout the week. And then I used that to justify having my work and pace of activity invade all seven days.

I quickly discovered that little breaks don't give you what a full, one-day break provides. You have to get the pace of life and work out of your system; you need to allow yourself to detach from it physically, emotionally, and mentally for a sustained period of time. Only then does the break really *give* you a break. That is why God says, "Not a little bit every day, but every seven days a *whole* day."

Which day you choose to take your rest is your call. The Sabbath was originally on Saturday, which is still the practice for

Jews. When Christianity began to spread, there was a movement toward Sunday as the day of rest, because that was the day that Jesus was resurrected. Except for a small handful of denominations, this has been the tradition and practice of Christians for two thousand years. But which day of the week you use for the Sabbath isn't as important as having a day of the week that you *use* for the Sabbath. The point is to get into the rhythm of a weekly rest. For many of us, it will be Sunday.[12] But setting aside that day will be an act of the will. It won't come naturally or easily. It's something that you are going to have to be intentional about.

Rest

Second, *rest* on that day. Make it a true Sabbath, which means make it a day in which you don't work! Now for you workaholics, let me be clear. A day of rest means that you don't use the break from work to read books about your work, and you don't use the day to plan out another week's worth of work. Don't touch work or anything to do with work with a ten-foot pole! And that doesn't just mean office work, but the kind of labor that is part of the day-in, day-out routine that fills your life. Washing clothes, mopping the floor, running errands—be careful here! You can stay away from work related to your vocation and simply fill it with *other* kinds of work! And that's what a lot of us do with our weekends— we may not work at the office or bring any work home with us, but we cram our weekends full of errands and tasks and chores that make what we do on Monday look tame!

When the Bible says to take a day to rest, it means to take a day to rest. To stop. To quit.

Sometimes I wonder if we know what a day like that would look like. I found out one January when the city of Charlotte was hit by a severe winter storm that practically shut down the city. We were one of thousands who lost power, and the ice and snow made going anywhere out of the question. We couldn't wash clothes, do dishes, run the microwave, turn on the TV, or work on the computer—everything that we might have used to fill our time or to work was taken away from us.

We were forced to stop!

We spent that day experiencing a *real* Sabbath rest—maybe the first in our family's life. It was great! But it only got better. As night approached, our power still hadn't come on. We decided that facing the frozen roads was better than staying in a frozen house, so we inched along abandoned, snow-covered roads to a hotel in a part of town that had power and spent the night there.

And we had a blast! We ordered pizza and watched movies and played in the indoor pool. To this day, our kids still talk about it. Whenever it's cold and the forecast calls for ice or snow, they all start hoping that our power will go out again. Why? Because when you take a day and make it a Sabbath—which means you really *stop*—another world opens up, one that puts more into you than you could possibly imagine.

Renew Yourself

Use your Sabbath as a day of renewal. Do something on that day that puts gas in your tank. If it's sailing, *sail.* If it's golfing, *golf.* If it's jogging, walking, renting a video, playing tennis, reading, sewing, gardening, or biking, *do it!*

I know that many of you may have a hard time with this, having grown up in a home or heritage that would consider such pursuits in violation of the spirit of God's directives. A man in seventeenth-century Scotland was once hauled into court just for *smiling* on the Sabbath.[13] In Jesus' time, the Pharisees had made a list of 1,521 things that you were not supposed to do on the Sabbath.[14] But Jesus didn't teach that, and neither does the Bible. In fact, the Bible records that one day, on the Sabbath, Jesus did one of the things that the Pharisees had on their list. He picked grain from a field for a meal. The Pharisees jumped all over Him, saying, "Why are You violating the Sabbath?" Note what Jesus said to them: "People were not made for the good of the Sabbath. The Sabbath was made for the good of people" (Mark 2:27 CEV).

God gave us the fourth commandment to restore us, not to frustrate us. It was never meant to be restrictive, unpleasant, or boring. It's supposed to be a day to look forward to—one that is renewing and inspiring. Some people have made it a day like hell instead of what it was meant to be—a day like heaven! So do whatever fills up your tank—cut your grass, cook out, take your boat out on the lake—whatever *renews* you.

Reflect

Finally, take some time to reflect, because your renewal needs to be physical, emotional, *and* spiritual. Work and busyness and fast-paced schedules keep us from reflection, from addressing the deep issues of our lives. That's why God says, "Be still, and know that I am God" (Ps. 46:10). How do you know God? You have to be *still*.

You have to stop long enough to let God speak to you, to reveal Himself to you, to be with you. To make a day a *Sabbath*, you have to include time for God. You have to bring God *into* your time-out. This is why from day one Christians have gathered for worship and teaching and fellowship with each other as part of the Sabbath. And this is why the Bible says, "Some people have gotten out of the habit of meeting for worship, but we must not do that" (Heb. 10:25 CEV).

The investment of worship helps you reflect and draw near to God. And if you throw in some rest from work and some renewal from recreation on that day, and if you do it every seven days—you've got the gift of God's fourth commandment.

And it's a gift we need.

CHAPTER 5

Honoring Your Parents

T im Berners-Lee is a proud father. His child has grown up to become one of the most well-known, powerful, successful beings on the planet. His offspring? The Internet. Tim Berners-Lee invented the World Wide Web, forever changing the shape of modern life and altering the way people do business, entertain and inform themselves, build communities, and exchange ideas. He continues to facilitate the Web's growth and development as the director of the World Wide Web Consortium and from his position at the MIT Laboratory for Computer Science.[1] I'll bet many of you did not even know his name until now. Yet his offspring belongs alongside Gutenberg's press, Bell's telephone, and Marconi's radio.

Tim is given little honor for his parenting role. Not quite right, is it? For those of us who benefit from the existence of the Web, he deserves a little gratitude and respect. But the overlooking of parents of ideas, patents, tools, and machines is nothing compared to the ambivalence often shown to biological parents. In truth, *ambivalence* isn't the right word. Try *rebellion*. And later on, for many, *resentment*. So the fifth commandment is nothing less than brazen to our ears: "Honor your father and your mother" (Exod. 20:12), which means treat them with respect: see them and treat them as people of worth and value.

WHY IT'S ON THE LIST

There are two basic reasons why God put honoring your parents on His top-ten list. The first is for your kids, and the second is for yourself.

Your children need to be taught to honor you and to respect you, because that honor and respect are the basis for their attitudes toward authority in general. If a child doesn't honor his or her parents, then he or she doesn't learn to work with authority anywhere else: with teachers, coaches, employers, and ultimately, God.

I was listening to public radio one day and heard an interview with a juvenile court judge. He said that in his court, he had seen violent juvenile crimes increase two to three times during recent years. The reporter asked him what he thought was causing the increased violence. He replied, "First, kids lost the *admiration* of authority. Then, they lost *respect* for authority. Now, they've lost the *fear* of authority."

But God doesn't just have this on His list for your kids' benefit; He has it on the list for *you*. How you choose to honor your parents will determine how you will be honored yourself.

One of Grimm's fairy tales tells of an old man who lived with his son, the son's wife, and the young couple's four-year-old boy. The old man's eyes blinked, and his hands shook. When he ate, the silverware rattled against the plate, and he often missed his mouth. Then the food would dribble onto the tablecloth. This upset the young mother, because she didn't want to have to deal with the extra mess and hassle of taking care of the old man. But he had nowhere else to live. So the young parents decided to move him away from the table, into a corner, where he could sit on a stool and eat from a bowl. And so he did, always looking at the table and wanting to be with his family but having to sit alone in the corner. One day his hands trembled more than usual; he dropped his bowl, and it broke. "If you are a pig," they said, "then you must eat out of a trough." So they made the old man a little wooden trough and put his meals in it.

Not long after, the couple came upon their four-year-old son playing with some scraps of wood. His father asked him what he was doing. The little boy looked up, smiled, and said, "I'm making a trough, to feed you and Mamma out of when I get big." The next day the old man was back at the table eating with the family, from a plate, and no one ever scolded him or mistreated him again.[2]

One day how we have honored our parents will all come back to us. One day we will be in need of our children's honor, and whether or not they demonstrate that honor will be up to us. I don't know about you, but I think God knew exactly what He was doing when He put this on His list—not only for the sake of our kids, but also for our own sake.

How to Honor Your Parents

So how do you begin honoring your parents? Let me throw out three ways, starting with the easiest one first.

Teach Your Children to Honor You

First, teach your kids to honor you. When they are very young, they learn this by *obeying* you. And your children learn to obey you through *discipline*. Nothing disturbs me more deeply than seeing a child showing disrespect for his or her mother or father. The mother tells them to do something, and they say, "No!" or "I hate you!" Everything in me wants to walk over and say, "Listen here, bucko, don't you talk to your mother that way or you won't be able to sit down for a week!" And just as I start to go over to the kid, my wife grabs me and reminds me, "Jim, he's not ours!" And I reply, "Oh, yeah. You're off the hook this time, kid."

Children are *taught* to honor; they're *taught* to respect. When a child talks back to his mother, ignores her, or shows disrespect to her in some other way, the mother has permitted it. This is why the Bible says: "Discipline your son in his early years while there is hope. If you don't you will ruin his life" (Prov. 19:18 TLB), as well as "Don't hesitate to discipline a child. A good spanking won't kill him. As a matter of fact, it may save his life" (Prov. 23:13–14 TEV).

A few years ago, my then-three-year-old son Zachary was the recipient of the direct application of this Scripture. His mother told him to do something, and he said no.

First mistake.

She told him *again*, and he had the audacity to say, "Don't talk to me that way."

Second mistake.

I was in the next room, overhearing the whole thing.

Third strike—and he was *out*.

I went into the room, bent down to his level, and said, "Little man, don't you *ever* talk to your mother that way, do you hear me?"

"Yes sir."

And then he got a spanking. Sorry if that offends you, but that's what happened. And he knew *why*. I know that some of you don't agree with spanking. When I was a kid, I didn't either. I've changed my views as a parent. But the question isn't *how* you discipline as much as *that* you discipline. You just can't let that stuff go. Kids need to be taught to respect you. With our children, we even teach their respect in how they answer us—"yes sir" or "no ma'am."

Having said that, please understand that nowhere in this commandment is there room for tyranny or harsh abuse. The Bible gives very clear parameters. God never wanted the fifth commandment to be a license for abuse or oppression. Look at what the Bible teaches in Ephesians: "Children, obey your parents; this is the right thing to do. . . . Honor your father and mother. . . . And now a word to you parents. Don't keep on scolding and nagging your children, making them angry and resentful. Rather, bring them up with the loving discipline the Lord himself approves, with suggestions and godly advice" (6:1–4 TLB).

The goal is for parents to be loving, giving, conscientious authority figures whom children are taught to respect.

James Dobson tells a story about a ten-year-old boy named Robert who was a patient of a California pediatrician. When Robert was scheduled for a visit to the doctor's office, the news would spread like wildfire. Nurses would whisper to themselves, "Batten down the hatches—Robert is coming!" He was an undisciplined terror. He would come in and tear magazines out of the holders, throw trash all over the waiting room, and wreak havoc throughout the clinic. Each time, his mother would just helplessly moan, "Oh Robert, oh Robert." If the office staff corrected the boy in any way, he would bite, kick, and scream his way back to the seat.

During one of his examinations, the pediatrician noticed that Robert had several cavities. He needed to refer him to a dentist, but he didn't want to inflict one of his dentist friends with this holy terror. Then he remembered that one of his colleagues had an unusual rapport with children, so he decided to send Robert there. Robert saw his trip to the dentist as a new and exciting challenge in his ongoing battle of the wills. As he was ushered into the dentist's office, he announced that he was *not* going to get into the chair. The dentist said, "Robert, I'm not going to force you, but I want you to climb up into the chair."

Robert clenched his fists and screamed at him that he would not.

The dentist patiently explained that Robert needed to get into the chair in order to get his teeth fixed. Robert refused—again— loudly. Then Robert played his trump card: "And if you come over here and try to make me, I'll take off all my clothes." The dentist looked over at his assistant, back over at Robert, and then simply said, "Fine. You go right ahead."

Robert did. He removed his shirt, undershirt, shoes, and socks, and then he stood defiantly in his Fruit of the Looms and looked at the dentist in a pose of victory.

"All right, son," the dentist said, "now get in that chair."

"You didn't hear me," said Robert, "I said that if you make me get on that chair, I will take off *all* my clothes!"

The doctor did not back down. So Robert continued to remove his clothes until he was as naked as the day he was born.

"Now," said the dentist, "get in that chair."

This time Robert did as he was told. No crying, no hitting, no kicking, and no biting. When the cavities were drilled and filled, Robert climbed down and asked for his clothes. The dentist said, "No, son, I'm not going to give them to you. You can tell your mother that we're going to keep your clothes tonight. She can pick them up tomorrow."

So out came Robert from the dentist's office into the waiting room to a very shocked mother. But she didn't say a word! She just took him by the hand, led him down the hall, and walked him right out into the parking lot to their car.

The next day the mother came for her son's clothes and asked to speak to the dentist. When he came out, she said, "Doctor, I want to thank you for what you did to Robert yesterday. For as long as I can remember, he has threatened us with just about everything. But his favorite has been that he'll take off his clothes if he doesn't get his way. You're the first person who has ever called his bluff, and he's already become a different child!"[3]

If authority and honor are not established, the consequences can be frightening. I read of a mother who went to a family therapist over her thirteen-year-old son who was rebelling in every way imaginable. Out every night until 2:00 A.M. and in trouble at school, her son was on a one-way course to self-destruction. The therapist asked if she could remember when it all started, and she could. It went back to when her son was less than three years old. She carried him into his room one night and put him in his crib, and he spit in her face. She told him not to do that, but he did it again. So she wiped her face off and tried to explain again, but then he spit on her face a third time. She didn't know what to do, so she just left him there and ran out of the room. He spit on the back of the door as she left. She never had the upper hand with her child after that night.[4]

Treat Your Parents with Respect

The second way to put the fifth commandment into your life is to treat *your* parents with respect. In your conversations and interactions with them, treat them with honor.

Most of us go through four stages with our parents:

1. First, we *idolize* our parents. They can do no wrong. Daddy is superman, and Mom is superwoman. That lasts about seven or eight years. It goes away when you have to cheat on games like *GeoSafari* or *Monopoly* in order to win.

2. Then comes adolescence, in which we tend to *demonize* our parents. They become the source of all of our misery, embodying all that we can and cannot do. If before they could do no wrong, now they can do no right.

3. Then we enter the stage in which we *utilize* our parents. It's "Can I borrow the car?" and "Can you pay for college?"

4. In the fourth stage, we *humanize* them. We see them like we see ourselves—with good points and bad points, strengths and weaknesses.[5]

It's when we face our parents' bad points that the call to honor gets sticky. There's no problem with raising our kids to respect us, but giving respect to *our parents* is another deal. The fifth commandment is not qualified. It doesn't say, "Honor your parents if they are honorable" or, "Treat them with respect if they are respectable." It simply says, "Honor your father and your mother."

And that's a bombshell.

Many of us carry around deep wounds from our parents, such as disappointment, rejection, pain, and hurt from a lack of love or affection. Some of us have even experienced physical or sexual abuse at the hands of our parents. So what is God asking you to do? Is He asking you to just forget about your pain? To put on a phony, plastic smile and go out and buy Hallmark cards, sending them off with a "hugs-and-kisses" signature? Is He asking you to gloss it all over or just to write it off?

Not on your life.

God doesn't want you to hide or deny your pain. He wants you to own it, identify it, and grieve over it. He wants you to address it head-on in whatever way it takes to end the cycle of pain. If you don't address your hurt, then you will harbor bitterness, anger, and resentment for the rest of your life.

The call to honor is the call to be healed from the scars you carry, and then from that healing, to be able to authentically honor your parents by seeing the good that is present in their lives. If you are not able to extend basic respect and honor to your mother or your father, then you haven't forgiven them, or you haven't faced the pain in a way that has brought resolution. Whatever pain they brought to you is still wounding you—through anger, resentment, bitterness, or even by repeating the same patterns with your own kids.

Few songwriters have been as candid in this area as Bruce Springsteen. On records and in concerts, he has shared openly about his difficult relationship with his father and the healing he has sought from those wounds. Perhaps the most poignant expression of all was found in "Independence Day," a song from his recording *The River*.

> Well Papa go to bed now it's getting late
> Nothing we can say is gonna change anything now
> I'll be leaving in the morning from St. Mary's Gate
> We wouldn't change this thing even if we could somehow
>
> 'Cause the darkness of this house has got the best of us
> There's a darkness in this town that's got us too
> But they can't touch me now
> And you can't touch me now
> They ain't gonna do to me
> What I watched them do to you

So say goodbye it's Independence Day
It's Independence Day
All down the line
Just say goodbye it's Independence Day
It's Independence Day this time

Now I don't know what it always was with us
We chose the words, and yeah, we drew the lines
There was just no way this house could hold the two of us
I guess that we were just too much of the same kind[6]

When God calls us to honor our parents, He knows that He is calling us to find release from whatever pain we experienced in our upbringing. He's calling us to find forgiveness and healing and release.

"But you don't know what they did to me!"

No, I don't. And you don't know what my parents did to me. But when God put this command on His list, He knew that every parent in the world would be a sinner. He knew that there would never be such a thing as a perfect father or a perfect mother. God doesn't want us to honor their sins or mistakes or weaknesses. He knows what went on. But He does want us to confront it, deal with it, and heal from it in such a way that we can then honor the fact that they were the ones who gave us life. You can disagree with them and reject any patterns of abuse or manipulation, but do so with *respect*.

Give Support to Your Parents

Finally, put the fifth commandment into your life by being willing to extend tangible support to your parents. The Bible says, "Take care of any widow who is really in need. But if a widow has children or grandchildren, they should learn to serve God by taking care of her, as she once took care of them. This is what God wants them to do. . . . People who don't take care of their relatives, and especially their own families, have given up their faith" (1 Tim. 5:3–4, 8 CEV). That's about as strong of a statement as you could make. If you don't honor your parents by caring for them, then it's as if God isn't in your life at all.

Jesus modeled for us the depth of this commitment. Look at what Jesus did when He was on the cross: "Near the cross of Jesus stood his mother. . . . When Jesus saw his mother there, and the disciple whom he loved standing nearby, he said to his mother, 'Dear woman, here is your son,' and to the disciple, 'Here is your mother.' From that time on, this disciple took her into his home" (John 19:25–27). Even though He was at the point of death, Jesus' commitment to honor His parents was so important that He made sure that His mother was cared for.

There is an increasing callousness and frightening lack of compassion in our society toward the elderly. Our culture is beginning to feel as if older people are expendable, which has resulted in a lack of responsibility. In addition, we are faced with the increasingly popular idea that all of our problems go back to how we were raised. So we vilify our parents and make them the source of all of our dysfunction. *They're* why I'm hurting, *they're* why my marriage failed, and *they're* why I'm so unhappy. Then comes the time when we as children assume the role of parents, and our parents assume the role of children. They're vulnerable, they're needy, and we have power over them. God says that at that moment, we should honor them. It may mean financial support as they grow old and need help with primary care and health-related costs. It may mean taking them into our homes or providing homes for them. Each situation is different, but the principle is clear: Honoring our parents means tangibly caring for them at their points of need.

At the state university I attended, I knew a history professor who was a Christian. He would go down to a local nursing home and visit with the elderly men and women there on a weekly basis. Though some were lovingly visited every day by their families—having been sent there because they needed care that couldn't be provided in a home environment—for many it was a place where they had been dumped so that their children wouldn't have to bother with them.

They were sad, and they were lonely.

One day, after this professor had made his weekly visit to those elderly people, a student stopped him and told him how wonderful it was that he had the love and a gift for "that sort of thing."

The professor was taken aback at the compliment. "A love for it? A gift for it? Do you think I enjoy smelling urine, stepping over bedpans, or talking with someone who drifts off into senile daydreams in the middle of a sentence? Enjoy it? You've got to be kidding!"

Now it was the student's turn to be stunned. "Then why do you go out there every week?"

"Because," the professor answered, "that is where Christ would be, and that is what Christ would do. And I am a follower of Christ."

By a Parent's Side

During the Vietnam War, near Father's Day, an elderly man collapsed on a Chicago street and was taken to the emergency room. He had no identification except for an old, smudged letter in his pocket. It was from his son, a soldier by the name of Jim Bates. You could tell the old guy had reread it hundreds of times. It practically fell apart in the nurse's hands. One of the orderlies contacted the Red Cross, and their sources located Private Bates at a military base in Kentucky. He caught the next plane to Chicago. No one thought his father would make it.

When the soldier arrived, they ushered him immediately into his father's room. He pulled up a straight chair next to the hospital bed. As he gripped the old man's limp hand, you could see constant squeezes of love and encouragement. One of the nurses offered to give the soldier a break from his bedside vigil, but he said softly, "Thank you, no. This is where I want to be."

The next morning, the father died. A nurse touched the soldier's arm and said, "I'm so sorry."

Then the soldier asked a question that shocked the entire ward. "Who was that man I was with?"

"He was your father, wasn't he?"

"No, he wasn't. I never saw him before in my life," the soldier replied. "When I first set eyes on him, I knew there had been a mistake. Then I realized he was too sick to tell whether or not I was his real son. I figured he needed me, so I stayed."

And with that, the soldier turned and left, giving everyone a lesson on what it means to honor a father and a mother—not necessarily for who they are, but for *what* they are.

CHAPTER 6

Respecting Human Life

A few years ago, a story appeared on the evening news that shocked even the most hardened of observers. More than thirty boys, most under the age of sixteen, embarked on an evening of activities they called "wilding." In their night on the town, they raped and nearly battered to death a twenty-eight-year-old woman who was jogging in Central Park in New York City. They hit her with a pipe, hacked her skull and thighs with a knife, pounded her face with a brick, and then bound her hands beneath her chin with her bloody sweatshirt, which also served as a gag. Then at least seven of the boys raped her. She lay undiscovered for almost four hours, losing three-quarters of the blood in her body.

One of the boys was asked why they had committed such an atrocity on another human being. "It was something to do," he replied with a smirk. "It was fun."

Our ability to manifest callous indifference to fellow human life can be chilling. In pre-Nazi Germany it was a common saying that "the human body contains a sufficient amount of fat to make seven cakes of soap, enough iron to make a medium-sized nail, a sufficient amount of phosphorus to equip two thousand match-heads, enough sulphur to rid one's self of one's fleas."[1] During the war, Himmler told his SS generals, "Whether the other nations live in prosperity or starve to death interests me only in so far as we need them as slaves for our culture. . . . Whether ten thousand Russian females fall down from exhaustion while digging an anti-tank ditch or not interests me only in so far as the anti-tank ditch for Germany is finished."[2]

THE SANCTITY OF HUMAN LIFE

Human life is sacred. Every life is valuable and irreplaceable. In Genesis, the Bible says, "God created man in his own image, in the image of God he created him; male and female he created them" (1:27). The fact that we were created in the image of God gives each and every one of us infinite worth and value. Taking it upon ourselves to end a life is the ultimate act of defiance against God, for life is His alone to give and take. It doesn't matter what the so-called "quality of life" is for that person. It doesn't matter what the cost of his or her life will be to society. It doesn't matter how productive, smart, or beautiful he or she is. It doesn't matter whether we like that person or not. All human beings have infinite worth because all human beings are made in the image of God. Thus the taking of a life—any life—is showing contempt for God and His image. As C. S. Lewis observed, "There are no *ordinary* people.

74

You have never talked to a mere mortal. Nations, cultures, arts, civilizations—these are mortal, and their life is to ours as the life of a gnat. But it is immortals whom we joke with, work with, marry, snub, and exploit. . . . Next to the Blessed Sacrament itself, your neighbour is the holiest object presented to your senses."[3]

In a scene from the movie *Ironweed*, the characters played by Jack Nicholson and Meryl Streep stumble across an old Eskimo woman lying in the snow, probably drunk. A bit tipsy themselves, the two enter into a debate as to what they should do about her.

"Is she drunk or a bum?" asks Nicholson.

"Just a bum. Been one all her life."

"And before that?"

"She was a whore in Alaska."

"She hasn't been a whore all her life. Before that?"

"I dunno. Just a little kid, I guess."

"Well, a little kid's something. It's not a bum and it's not a whore. It's something. Let's take her in."

And that is the way God calls all of us to see others, through a lens not only of grace, but of value. Every man and woman is made in the image of God, no matter how defaced that image may be.[4] Human life, in every form, is holy ground.

THE SIXTH COMMANDMENT

In Exodus 20:13, God says, "You shall not murder." Notice that He does not say, "You shall not kill," but, "You shall not murder." He could have used another Hebrew word that was the more generic term "to kill," but this one is laser sharp: *murder,* the deliberate, willful, premeditated taking of a human life out of hatred, anger, greed, or self-centered convenience.[5] This command does not refer to the killing that takes place in war, in self-defense, or even in capital punishment. Those are important discussions, and the Bible has much to say about them, but they're not the focus of the sixth commandment. Nor does the sixth commandment speak to the killing of other creatures, such as animals. It is specific in its directive toward the willful murder of human beings.[6]

FIRST-DEGREE MURDER

Of all the commandments, this is the one that we have a tendency to feel the best about in terms of an authentic life of obedience. This is the one that lets us stand up and proudly say, "I'm with You, God—murder is horrible. I've *never* done it, and I think that those who *have* committed murder are reprehensible and deserve Your harshest judgment." Finally, a commandment whose obedience we can celebrate without awkwardness in regard to how we've lived our lives!

Can I share something with you? I'm a murderer. I've killed people. Can I share something else? I'll bet you have too. To experience an authentically spiritual life, you must stop your murderous lifestyle.

The Bible talks about the taking of a life in ways you may have never imagined; in each situation, God looks down and sees an execution. Reflecting on the sixth commandment begins with what I'll call murder in the first degree, which can take place in at least five different ways.

Homicide

The first type of murder in the first degree is homicide. This is the kind of killing that probably came to your mind when you first read the sixth commandment. Our papers are filled with shootings, stabbings, and beatings that result in the death of one human being at the hands of another. And this kind of deliberate murder is a grievous thing in the eyes of God. The Bible records the very first murder, which took place when Cain killed his younger brother, Abel. It also records God's reaction: "The LORD said, 'Why have you done this terrible thing? Your brother's blood is crying out to me from the ground'" (Gen. 4:10 TEV).

It's easy to become numb to murder. Stories of brutal murders fill our news, and familiarity breeds inattention and indifference. Then something comes along that reminds us of its horror. Take, for example, the book *Lost Lives*, written over eight years by four journalists and totaling more than sixteen hundred pages. It's a comprehensive, gut-wrenching portrait of three decades of violence through brief biographies memorializing every victim of Northern Ireland's bloodshed, more than thirty-six hundred in all. Each year's list of dead is prefaced with quotes from witnesses and survivors, such as when Irish Republican Army dissidents killed twenty-nine people with a car bomb in Omagh in 1998. The mother of twelve-year-old James Barker recalls the scene in the town's emergency morgue: "To see him lying there, with half his head gone, and those beautiful green eyes looking out at me as if he was waiting for me, was devastating. I never realized how green his eyes were." By the authors' reckoning, anti-British militants killed 2,140 people, with 1,772 of those attributed to the dominant wing of the Irish Republican Army. The IRA's enemies in Protestant paramilitary groups killed 1,050 people, the British army killed 301, and the province's police forces killed 52. The other 94 deaths are attributed to mob violence. "This book is an enormous social commentary on our failure to organize the way we live together," said Maurice Hayes, a Belfast civil servant who helped provide funding for the project. "It should hold up a warning card to the community and say: What was it all for?"[7]

Suicide

But homicide is not the only kind of first-degree murder.[8] A logical extension of the sixth commandment also includes suicide—the murder of your own self. Christians have long held that suicide is morally wrong because they have seen it as a contradiction of our being creatures, as opposed to the Creator. Suicide shakes its fist at God and refuses to receive life moment by moment from His hand. The person who commits suicide takes life as his or her own possession.[9]

Because of the severity of the "independence" of suicide in relation to the sovereignty of God, some have viewed suicide as an unforgivable sin. While it is unclear what the consequences of suicide might be in the eyes of God, the Bible doesn't say anything about suicide being the unforgivable sin or an act that commits you to hell. Yet it is clearly the wrongful taking of a life and a violation of the sixth commandment.

Infanticide

A third form of murder is infanticide, the ending of the life of a child, usually because the child carries a physical or mental defect. As shocking as that might sound, infanticide is a growing phenomenon in our country. Consider the views of Peter Singer, an Australian bioethicist who maintains, "When the death of a disabled infant will lead to the birth of another infant with better prospects of a happy life, the total amount of happiness will be greater if the disabled infant is killed."[10]

One of the most celebrated cases of infanticide took place in 1982 when a baby boy known only as Baby Doe was born with Down syndrome and a badly formed esophagus. The esophagus problem could have been easily corrected by a routine operation. Yet because their child had Down syndrome, the parents refused permission to operate. They also ordered that their son not be given food or water. Pediatricians pleaded with the parents to allow them to operate and to feed their child. They pointed out that persons with Down syndrome had happy and productive lives. Other couples offered to adopt the baby. Before an appeal could be lodged with the Supreme Court, Baby Doe died of starvation.[11]

Compare this to the young boy born in 1975 and given the name of Raymond Dunn Jr. You may know him by his more famous title: the Gerber Boy. At the time of his birth, he experienced an accidental skull fracture and oxygen deprivation that caused severe retardation. As he grew, other problems developed. His twisted body would go through up to twenty seizures a day. He was blind, mute, and immobile. He also had severe allergies that limited him in a bizarre way to one and only one food: a meat-based formula made by Gerber Foods. But in 1985, Gerber stopped making that formula. So Raymond's mother started scouring the country to buy everything stores still had in stock. In spite of her efforts, by 1990, her supply ran out. She went to Gerber and told them of her situation—that without their help, Raymond would die.

Here's what Gerber did.

Employees donated hundreds of hours of volunteer time to bring out old equipment, set up production lines, obtain special approval from the USDA, and produce the old formula—all for one little boy. Little Raymond died in January 1995, but the day-in, day-out commitment of the Gerber employees gave him and his family five precious years of life—years that mattered, because *Raymond* mattered.[12]

Euthanasia

Another extension of the sixth commandment is euthanasia, which has received an enormous amount of media attention in recent years. Euthanasia is assisted suicide, usually because the person is old, in pain, or terminally ill. The word *euthanasia* is derived from two Greek words: *eu*, which means "good," and *thanatos*, which means "death." So the word *euthanasia* literally means "good death."

Those who support euthanasia use terms trying to support this sentiment, such as "mercy killing" and "death with dignity." The rationale is that individuals or family members have the right to end their own or someone else's life if they feel it seems unbearable. This isn't the question of whether or not to use extraordinary means to extend the process of dying when there is no hope for extending life, which is often called *passive* euthanasia. What we are talking about is the direct killing of a patient because a disease may be terminal or the withholding of assistance that would prolong life in a substantive way simply to avoid pain or difficulty. Euthanasia is every bit as much the taking of a human life as any other means of murder, because regardless of your intentions, it's not your life to take.

Abortion

The fifth way that we can directly and purposefully end a human life is easily one of the most morally divisive issues in our country today—abortion. On January 22, 1973, the Supreme Court made a decision that has come to be known simply as *Roe v. Wade*, which legalized a woman's right to an abortion. Since that ruling, America has averaged more than one-and-one-half million abortions every year. That is close to five thousand babies a *day!* Ninety-seven percent of all abortions are performed for the purpose of birth control—not because of rape, incest, or because the mother's life is in danger, but because the baby was simply unwanted, inconvenient, or unplanned.

Most of the rhetoric surrounding the abortion issue—on both

sides—is completely out of sync with the spirit of Christ. As a result, reasoned dialogues are few and far between. Without inflammatory language, let me share my heart with you on this issue.

Everything that makes up a human being is present at conception. When the sperm and egg come together, all forty-six chromosomes that form our genetic code are present. From that point on, it is only a question of development. As early as twenty-one days, before the woman even knows she is pregnant, the child's first heartbeats begin. By the fifth month, the baby has hair on his head, eyebrows and eyelashes, and nails on his fingertips. By the sixth month, the baby can cry, suck his thumb, and make a fist. He can even open his eyelids and grip things. No wonder the psalmist wrote this praise to God:

> For you created my inmost being; you knit me together in my mother's womb. I praise you because I am fearfully and wonderfully made; your works are wonderful, I know that full well. My frame was not hidden from you when I was made. . . . When I was woven together . . . your eyes saw my unformed body. All the days ordained for me were written in your book before one of them came to be. (Ps. 139:13–16)

I know that the great argument in favor of abortion is that a woman has the right to choose, the right to govern her body. But that reasoning is only true if the child in her body isn't a life in the eyes of God. But the child in her womb *is* a life in the eyes of God. And we are not God—our unborn child's life is not up to us to end.

I cannot begin to tell you the level of compassion I have for those of you who have had an abortion and carry around deep wounds of regret and guilt. I so want you to know that God loves you, that you matter to Him, and that you can find forgiveness in Christ for whatever choices you have made. But with equal feeling, I need to say that abortion is a great evil.

I'll never forget when Mother Teresa was the keynote speaker at the 1994 National Prayer Breakfast in Washington. She was eighty-three years old at the time and had to be rolled to the platform in a wheelchair. At four-foot-six, she barely peeked over the podium. Yet during that address, she spoke as if she were ten feet tall with words that resounded in the hearts of everyone present: "If we accept that a mother can kill even her own child," she implored, "how can we tell other people not to kill each other?" Then she pleaded with pregnant women who might be thinking about abortion. "Please don't kill the child. I want the child. Please give me the child. I want it. I will care for it."[13] That was true. At that point in time, she had personally taken and placed more than three thousand unwanted children into loving homes. Why? Because she knew that each life mattered to God.

And that conviction is the basis for obeying God's sixth commandment—a deep, inner conviction that life is sacred. And sometimes that conviction can only come when you are faced with its cheapening. One of the greatest advocates for the sanctity of human life has been Pope John Paul II. The character of the man known during his youth as Karol Wojtyla was forged in the fire of Poland during World War II, in which six million Polish citizens out of a prewar

population of thirty-five million were either killed in combat or mur-
dered. Poland also became the sight of the greatest slaughters of the
Holocaust. No wonder he was the pope who delivered the forty-
eight-thousand-word encyclical, *Evangelium Vitae*—"The Gospel of
Life"—which he signed on March 25, 1995, on the Feast of the
Annunciation, the solemn annual celebration of the Incarnation of
the Son of God who entered history as an unborn child.[14]

SECOND-DEGREE MURDER

But there is another way of killing that the Bible also talks about
with great seriousness. We'll call it murder in the *second*-degree.[15]
This category comes straight from the teaching of Jesus, lifted
from His most famous sermon—the Sermon on the Mount:
"You're familiar with the command . . . 'Do not murder.' I'm
telling you that anyone who is so much as angry with a brother or
sister is guilty of murder. Carelessly call a brother 'idiot!' and you
just might find yourself hauled into court. Thoughtlessly yell 'stupid!' at a sister and you are on the brink of hellfire. The simple
moral fact is that words kill" (Matt. 5:21–22 MSG).

I don't know about you, but I find Jesus very uncomfortable
here. I am more at ease with what Will Campbell records a
Louisiana minister musing, "I don't hate anybody. 'Cause the
Bible says it's a sin to hate. But there are some folks I hope dies of
cancer of the tonsils."[16] Yet Jesus reminds me that my biting words,
my character assassinations, slander, innuendo, gossip, and snide
remarks are every bit as revolting to the eyes and heart of God as
the dripping knife and the smoking gun.[17]

When a parent tells a child that he or she is stupid, ugly, or worthless, a little part of that child dies. When you go on the warpath against another person, becoming active in ruining his or her reputation, spreading accusations, criticizing his or her behavior, or taking verbal shots, you are taking a gun and emptying its contents in that person's direction. It's an assault with the intent to kill. The Bible is very clear on this—take a look at the directness found in the Book of James: "A word out of your mouth may seem of no account, but it can accomplish nearly anything—or destroy it! . . . By our speech we can . . . throw mud on a reputation. . . . The tongue runs wild, a wanton killer. . . . With our tongues we . . . curse the very men and women [God] made in his image. . . . My friends, this can't go on" (3:5–10 MSG).

No wonder missionary Amy Carmichael hung a sign in the dining room of her home in Dohnavur, India, that read: "May the absent one always be safe at our table!"[18]

There's a story from the Solomon Islands in the South Pacific regarding a unique form of logging practiced by the villagers. If a tree is too large to be felled with an ax, the natives cut it down by yelling at it. Woodsmen credited with special powers creep up on a tree at dawn and then scream at the tree at the top of their lungs. They continue this for thirty days. The tree, it is told, then dies and falls over. The villagers base their practice on the belief that hollering kills the spirit of the tree. According to the villagers, it always works. I don't know if their practice works on trees, but I do know that it works on people.[19]

Ask Amy Hagadorn.

When she was only nine years old, little Amy made national news

85

because of a letter she wrote to Santa Claus. She didn't ask for a Barbie or a stocking full of toys. All she asked for was a day at school that she wouldn't be teased. Amy had cerebral palsy, which is a disorder of the nervous system that caused her to walk with a limp, have limited use of her right hand, and impaired speech. In her letter to Santa, Amy wrote, "Kids laugh at me because of the way I walk and run and talk. I just want one day where no one laughs at me or makes fun of me." Then she added words that bring back painful memories for many of us: "It's especially bad at gym and recess." A radio station got hold of Amy's letter, and their report brought national media attention. As a result, her hometown of Fort Wayne, Indiana, declared the Tuesday before Christmas "Amy Day."[20]

But they could have just called it "Respect Human Life" day. That's the challenge of the sixth commandment: *Respect human life.* In *whatever* form you find it—your neighbor, a stranger, a child, an elderly person, someone with Down syndrome, the unborn, the person who wronged you, or someone you are angry with. Respect human life! It has value and importance in *any* and *every* form.

REASON ENOUGH

The *Charlotte Observer* ran a story in the late nineties about another little girl whose name was also Amy—Amy Wooten. Only four years old, she had acute leukemia and needed a bone marrow transplant. The family and doctors issued word throughout the Charlotte area, and on the Saturday designated for testing, something happened that was almost beyond belief. More than two thousand people were standing in line to get their blood typed for a possible match. When asked why, two students who had come down from Appalachian State University said, "A four year old child is reason enough."[21]

That is what the sixth commandment is all about—respecting human life.

CHAPTER 7

Staying Faithful

Francesca Johnson was a Midwestern woman who lived on an Iowa farm with her husband and two children. Her husband and children were getting ready to leave the farm for the Illinois State Fair, where they intended to exhibit a prize steer.

They were going to be away for a week.

Within hours of their departure, a national magazine photographer, Robert Kincaid, drove into the farmyard. He told Francesca that he was in the area to photograph the covered bridges of Iowa's Madison County, was a bit lost, and could use some directions. They talked and shared a cool drink, leading to a second visit and the acceptance of a casual dinner invitation. That led to a longer conversation, a dance, and then a cascade into a passionate love affair.

You are probably among the millions familiar with this story, made famous in the best-selling novel *The Bridges of Madison County*. Unfortunately, it's a tale that runs headlong into the seventh commandment of God.

THE SEVENTH COMMANDMENT

In Exodus 20:14, God says, "You shall not commit adultery." The word *adultery* simply refers to sex that is outside of the marriage covenant, something many people evidently feel led to pursue, for the latest research shows that at least 60 percent of all marriages will be affected by an affair.[1]

Contrary to what the world says, God commands us to stay faithful to our spouses and not to go outside of the marital relationship for any form of sexual expression for any reason. Or, as it is phrased in the Book of Proverbs, "Drink from your own well, my son—be faithful and true to your wife. . . . Rejoice in the wife of your youth. Let her charms and tender embrace satisfy you. Let her love alone fill you with delight. . . . *For God is closely watching you,* and he weighs carefully everything you do" (5:15–21 TLB).

BUT WHY?

Some of you might be wondering why God thinks adultery is such a big deal. Especially today, when sex before marriage, as well as outside of marriage, is not only common, but valued. An article in *Glamour* magazine told of a father who intentionally drove his daughter and her boyfriend to a hotel for the express purpose of losing her virginity. The title of the article was "My Girlfriend's Father—What a Man!"[2] In such a climate, it's no wonder that a wife went to lunch with eleven other women, and when one woman asked, "How many of you have been faithful throughout your marriage?" only one hand was raised. Relaying the scene to her husband, the wife confessed that she was not the one who had raised her hand. She quickly added, "But don't worry. I've been faithful to you." When the husband asked why she hadn't ventured her fidelity to the other women, she responded, "I was ashamed."[3]

Today, sexual activity outside of marriage has changed from being adultery to an "affair," a word full of mystery, excitement, and intrigue. It's a relationship, not a sin.[4] So why would God take relationships as beautiful and romantic as the kind that took place in *The Bridges of Madison County* or the movies *Titanic* and *Shakespeare in Love* and try to make it something bad? It's a fair question. There's also a fair answer. Let's walk through some of the reasons why God cares about adultery, because there is a dark side of adultery that is seldom discussed.

Adultery Destroys Emotional Union

First, adultery destroys the emotional union of your marriage. Look at what the apostle Paul wrote: "There's more to sex than mere skin on skin. Sex is as much spiritual mystery as physical fact. As written in Scripture, 'The two become one'" (1 Cor. 6:16 MSG). No other human activity has the same power as sexual intimacy. It is the supreme expression of a relationship. It is ultimate emotional unity. Because of that, it needs the safety and boundaries of marriage to protect it from wounding us deeply. That's why the Bible says, "We must not pursue the kind of sex that avoids commitment and intimacy, leaving us more lonely than ever—the kind of sex that can never 'become one'" (1 Cor. 6:17–18 MSG).

When you talk to people who have been wounded by an affair, you discover that it isn't just the physical dimension that wounds. It's the fact that they were deceived, that their mates were dishonest with them, that they were betrayed. When you commit adultery, you're not merely violating your marriage oath; you're violating another person. Dr. Frank Pittman, an Atlanta psychiatrist interviewed by *Newsweek* magazine for a cover story on adultery, said that adultery isn't about "whom you lie with. It's whom you lie to."[5] Adultery causes pain. It rips a family apart. People get hurt—*badly*. God gave us the seventh commandment because He wants to protect us from that hurt.

Adultery Is a Direct Offense against God

God also cares about our relationship with Him, and sexual sin is a direct offense against Him that separates us from His love.

God created us, and part of our creation was sexuality. When we misuse our bodies through inappropriate sexual behavior, it tears away at our soul and drives God away. The apostle Paul talked about this in 1 Corinthians: "There is a sense in which sexual sins are different from all others. In sexual sin we violate the sacredness of our own bodies, these bodies that were made for God-given and God-modeled love, for 'becoming one' with another. Or didn't you realize that your body is a sacred place, the place of the Holy Spirit?" (6:18–19 MSG).

But this command isn't limited simply to those who are married. This commandment is about any sexual activity outside of marriage—whether before marriage, after marriage, or outside of marriage. The Bible is not ambiguous in this area. "Honor marriage," writes the biblical author of Hebrews, "and guard the sacredness of sexual intimacy between wife and husband. God draws a firm line against casual and illicit sex" (13:4 MSG). God designed our sexual fulfillment to be expressed in the context of love, trust, and lifelong commitment. To engage in sex apart from marriage between a man and a woman tears apart the very nature of what God has designed for us as sexual creatures, and it attacks the foundation of our relationship with Him as Creator and Leader.

Adultery Leads to Sexually Transmitted Diseases

A third reason that God no doubt wants us to stay faithful to our spouses has to do with the physical repercussions of sexually transmitted diseases. Does the Bible ever record God saying, "Watch out for venereal disease"? No, but the following straightforward advice doesn't demand a degree in rocket science to apply: "Can you build a fire in your lap and not burn your pants? Can you walk barefoot on hot coals and not get blisters? . . . Adultery is a brainless act, soul-destroying, self-destructive" (Prov. 6:27–29, 32 MSG). There are twelve million cases of sexually transmitted diseases every year. The AIDS epidemic is reaching monstrous proportions, and efforts at making sure that we all wear condoms aren't going to safeguard anybody. The failure rate of condoms when it comes to preventing pregnancy is somewhere between 15 and 26 percent. And the HIV virus is 450 times smaller than sperm. God's call to remain faithful to our spouses protects us from the pain of such epidemics.

93

Fatal Attractions

A final reason that gives credence to God's warnings in the area of sexual intimacy is that sexual encounters outside of marriage are almost always fatal attractions. If you saw the movie by that name, you saw a vivid picture of just how fatal this type of attraction can be. But a destructive extramarital relationship is not just movie fiction; it can be reality. A therapist once wrote from her counseling practice about the ways affairs can end in complicated, difficult ways. One man's affair lasted fewer than two months. The woman he was involved with sent a copy of a sexually explicit love letter to his wife. The letter, which turned out to be a fake, also stated that he had never loved his wife and that he had had many other affairs.

In another relationship, a woman's lover contacted her *parents* and told them about the affair. He went into detail about how she had seduced him and tried to break up his marriage.

Then there was a man who only had sex with a particular woman on two occasions, but he contracted herpes, which he inadvertently passed onto his wife while she was pregnant.

Another woman never actually had sex with a certain man with whom she became emotionally involved, but he became infatuated and obsessed with her and now follows her everywhere. She is terrified of what he might do, but the police can't do anything because there hasn't been a crime.

Another man found out that the woman he was involved with became pregnant, even though she told him she was using a contraceptive. She had the baby and agreed to confidentiality in exchange for a one-time payment of seventy-five thousand dollars.

He paid the money, but then a year later, she turned around and filed a paternity suit.[6]

But these fatal attractions are not limited to marital affairs. Sex *before* marriage can be *equally* devastating. For example, sex before marriage can overwhelm the dating relationship. Physical intimacy becomes a substitute for emotional intimacy. Passion and stimulation get confused with love and commitment. And the sexual intimacy will dominate, which more often than not means that the infrastructure for a lasting relationship will not be built.

According to the research of sociologists from the University of Chicago and the University of Michigan, couples who live together before marriage are more likely to get a divorce than those who move in together after their vows. This is a direct contradiction to the idea that if you live together first, you'll be better prepared for marriage and therefore reduce the risk of divorce. The truth is that living together cheapens the value of the marriage covenant, giving each partner the impression that when the relationship is not as rewarding as he or she would like, moving out or breaking up is always an option.

Another consequence of sex before marriage is that it results in shame and alienation. You cannot walk away from sex unchanged. By joining your body with another's, you have entered into oneness with that person; the separation of the one back into two always leaves damage to the soul. That's why the Bible says, "The body is not meant for sexual immorality" (1 Cor. 6:13).

I once read of a young girl named Eve who could give firsthand testimony to this truth. She was a fifteen-year-old, straight-A student who was pretty, outgoing, and a leader in her youth group at church. One night she came home, did her homework, kissed her parents good-night, and went upstairs to bed. A few hours later, they found her stretched out on her bed in a white gown, hands folded, eyes closed, and wearing one black sock and one white sock.

An empty bottle of pills lay by her bed.

Thankfully, her suicide had been discovered in time. The emergency room at the hospital called for a counselor to talk to Eve. He asked her why she tried to kill herself and what she intended by wearing one black sock and one white sock.

Then her story came out.

He was an eighteen-year-old senior on the football team who paid attention to her and asked her out on a date. He kept after Eve, showering her with attention and making her feel special. He finally talked her into letting him drive her home from band practice. Instead, he drove to a secluded field. He started kissing her, touching her. She told him to stop, but he wouldn't, and she didn't know how to stop him.

After the sex, he drove her home. He had no boundaries, so he violated hers. Like so many others, he was blind to what his sexuality was doing to him or to anyone else.

Overcome by shame, guilt, and pain, Eve tried to take her life. Something deeply private and personal had been violated. Something special had been lost. She wasn't *one* anymore; she was divided and torn apart.

One white sock, and one black sock.[7]

So understand, God's design for sexual intimacy is for our *benefit*. The purpose of what the Bible has to say isn't to cramp your style or limit your pleasure, but to free you to experience sexual pleasure in a way that is unhindered from negative consequences.

THE STRAIGHT LIFE

So why do we refuse to obey the seventh commandment? Even when we know it's not best for us, countless numbers of us run toward sexual disobedience as fast as our legs will carry us. James Dobson gives great insight into this aspect of our nature, talking about it in terms of the "straight life."[8]

To illustrate, let's establish a line and call it the "straight life."

The Straight Life

The straight life is mowing the lawn, working almost fifty weeks a year, taking two or three weeks for vacation and probably giving that to the kids. It's spending money wisely when you'd rather buy a boat. It's going to work when you'd rather go fishing; it's being responsible, paying your taxes, and cleaning the garage. It's staying married to one woman in spite of temptations to do the opposite.

And let's be honest—the straight life gets heavy for *all* of us.

There are many voices calling us off of the straight life—more now than ever. Everywhere we go, we hear "You're number one,"

97

"Make yourself happy," "Don't let anybody cramp your style," "Go for the gusto," "Don't take it anymore," and "You only go around once." But within the chorus, there are four primary voices that tend to call people off of the straight life.

The first voice that calls us off the straight life is *pleasure*.

Pleasure

The Straight Life

Dobson tells of a high-school vice principal who ran off with his secretary. Dobson asked him, "Jack, why'd you do it? Why did you leave your wife and kids?" His friend was startlingly honest. "Well," he said, "two children were all I ever wanted. All I could afford, all I could handle, all I had time for. Then my wife had a dream she lost those kids, and she started hammering me for another. Well, we ended up with twins, and the fifth was an accident. Our house was constantly filled with noise and confusion. Every minute I had was being put into that responsibility. And quite frankly, fun and games looked pretty good to me."

A second voice that calls people off of the straight life is *romanticism*.

Pleasure

The Straight Life

Romanticism

Romanticism is the desire for "some enchanted evening," looking through the scrapbook and finding the pressed flower from your junior prom, wondering if somebody still cares, wondering if life is passing you by. Romanticism is what made Francesca Johnson dance with a visiting photographer on that fateful Iowa night.

A third voice is *sex.*

Pleasure

The Straight Life

Romanticism   *Sexual Gratification*

Sex is what usually gets the most credit for people leaving the straight life, and it is a powerful voice, particularly for men. But it's not really why we leave.

The real reason, the most powerful voice of all, hasn't even been raised—the voice of ego.

Pleasure   *Ego Needs*

The Straight Life

Romanticism   *Sexual Gratification*

The ego is the most powerful voice of all. It's the number one reason that people enter into an affair. It's the attention, the compliments, and discovering that someone of the opposite sex still finds you attractive and appealing. In the Bible, Solomon writes in the Book of Proverbs about a man who left his wife. In commenting about why, we read that "he yielded to her. He couldn't resist her flattery" (7:21 TLB).

LEAVING THE STRAIGHT LIFE

How do people leave the straight life? Do they do it all at once in a direct leap toward one of the four voices?

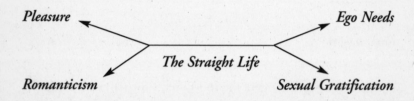

Not usually. More often than not, leaving the straight life is gradual. It occurs over time with little departures. A long lunch, an intimate conversation, and a drive home. Visually, it's more like this:

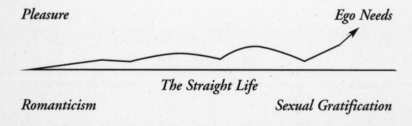

And what happens after somebody leaves? Do they live happily ever after? Here's a rude awakening—they simply establish another straight life. Romanticism tends to die down. Flaws come into

100

focus. You have your first fight. The sexual relationship loses its glamour and becomes routine. Thoughts eventually turn to earning a living and cooking and cleaning and paying taxes, and then the ego needs begin to accumulate just like they did before. No wonder research has shown that 80 percent of those who have an affair, get divorced, and marry the person they had an affair with later said that they wish they could go back to their original spouse. *Eighty percent.*[9]

STAYING FAITHFUL

So how do you experience an authentic life by staying faithful to your spouse and to God? How can you be sexually obedient outside of marriage? Here are some practical steps you can take.

Monitor and Control Your Thought Life

It's been noted that the most important sexual organ you have is your brain. Whoever made that remark was very, very wise. Jesus Himself said, "You have heard that it was said, 'Do not commit adultery.' But I tell you that anyone who looks at a woman lustfully has already committed adultery with her in his heart" (Matt. 5:27–28). Jesus wasn't talking about the first innocent look or the initial casual glance. Nor was He talking about the appreciation of someone's beauty. He was talking about the second, third, and fourth looks that are accompanied by an imagined seduction or liaison, the mental undressing, the conscious fantasy of having a sexual relationship. Moral failure almost always begins in our minds. You're in bed with someone mentally long before you are in bed with him or her physically.[10] So guard your mind, and do not let yourself engage in unchecked sexual fantasy.

Avoid Vulnerable or Compromising Situations

A second precaution to take is to be sure to avoid vulnerable or compromising situations. Let me get down to basics on this one, because it's important.

1. Watch how and when you are alone with someone of the opposite sex.

2. Watch how you touch people of the opposite sex—be careful with your hugs and lingering touches.

3. Don't drive someone of the opposite sex home or visit someone of the opposite sex alone at home.

4. Don't travel alone with someone of the opposite sex.

5. Watch out for that long lunch, that after-work drink, the moments when you stay late and work together on a project with someone of the opposite sex.

And if there is someone to whom you *know* you are attracted, be *particularly* on guard. If there is someone you think about a lot, catch yourself comparing your spouse to in an uncomplimentary way, find excuses to be with, or have sexual fantasies about, you are in the red zone. This is not a time for caution, but radical extradition. Flee! Remove yourself at once! Do *not* trust your own strength of will. It's like the war movie I once saw on late-night TV in which an entire squadron of soldiers was attacked and defeated by enemy troops because their sentries had fallen asleep. The enemy was able to sneak up on their camp inch by inch, yard by yard, and then totally overwhelm them. It is no different with sexual sin. If you don't set up guards and establish a defense to protect your heart and life, then you will be extremely vulnerable. The worst thing in the world you could believe is, "Aw, that's not a problem for me." If this is your mind-set, you are in a most dangerous position. You must intentionally set up barriers, no matter who you are or how strong you think you are.

Meet Your Spouse's Needs

Finally, for those of you who are married, do the hard work of meeting your spouse's needs. We are most vulnerable to an affair when we have physical or emotional needs that are not being met. If pleasure, romanticism, sexual gratification, and ego needs are the four voices that call us off of the straight life, then the key to preventing an affair is to work at bringing these four elements into your present marriage!

Reserve time for pleasure. Husbands and wives should go out on dates, explore recreational activities together, and do things together for sheer fun. In the Song of Solomon, we are allowed a glimpse inside a passionate love affair and discover one of its secrets: "This is my lover, this my friend" (Song of Sol. 5:16).

But that's not the only way to rekindle the passion in your relationship. Keep the romantic fires burning through love notes and surprises and candlelit dinners and unexpected weekend trips. Reserve time and energy for meaningful sexual activity, and work hard at fulfilling each other's sexual needs. And husbands and wives should work *overtime* at building each other's self-esteem, talking about how proud they are of each other and looking for ways to compliment each other. Love is more than a feeling; it requires care and discipline and investment.

See the Beauty of Marriage

Finally, see the *beauty* of the marriage covenant and be captured by its glory. Be moved by its nobility and taken by its grandeur.

David Ireland wrote a book titled *Letters to an Unborn Child.* Ireland was dying from a crippling neurological disease when he discovered that his wife was pregnant. Knowing that he would never see his own child, he took up his pen to write all that he would never have a chance to say. In those letters, he writes to his unborn child about his wife, the child's mother:

> Your mother is very special. Few men know what it's like
> to receive appreciation for taking their wives out to dinner
> when it entails what it does for us. It means that she has to
> dress me, shave me, brush my teeth, comb my hair; wheel
> me out of the house and down the steps, open the garage and

put me in the car, take the pedals off the chair, stand me up, sit me in the seat of the car, twist me around so that I'm comfortable, fold the wheelchair, put it in the car, go around to the other side of the car, start it up, back it out, get out of the car, pull the garage door down, get back into the car, and drive off to the restaurant.

And then, it starts all over again; she gets out of the car, unfolds the wheelchair, opens the door, spins me around, stands me up, seats me in the wheelchair, pushes the pedals out, closes and locks the car, wheels me into the restaurant, then takes the pedals off the wheelchair so I won't be uncomfortable. We sit down to have dinner, and she feeds me throughout the entire meal. And when it's over she pays the bill, pushes the wheelchair out to the car again, and reverses the same routine. And when it's over—finished—with real warmth she'll say, "Honey, thank you for taking me out to dinner."

I never quite know what to answer.[11]

IF YOU'VE ALREADY LEFT THE STRAIGHT LIFE

Before we leave this area, let me say a word to those of you who have been involved in an affair. There is nothing in the world that God would rather have happen than for you to come to Him, tell Him you're sorry, and be forgiven. God is in the business of second chances. In the Bible, through the prophet Isaiah, God said, "No matter how deep the stain of your sins, I can take it out and make you as clean as freshly fallen snow" (Isa. 1:18 TLB).

Take Him up on it.

And for those of you in the process of leaving the straight life or currently living in the abandonment of it, please, I beg you, think long and hard about what you are doing. Are you really on the path you *want* to be on, *need* to be on, or are *supposed* to be on? It's never too late to change your course, to alter your direction, or to start over. If you're in an affair right now, break it off. God will walk with you through it, and He'll honor every hard step you have to take along the way, from telling the truth to your spouse to returning to the life you left. Break it off. It's not worth it. You *can* obey God in this area, finding the authentic life you most deeply desire—one that is beautiful to behold.

CHAPTER 8

Acquiring by the Rules

Our first home in Charlotte was rented, due to the fact that we came to the city as a church planter. Translation: We were very, very poor. Though we were thankful for any home, the house wasn't much to look at and offered fewer than nineteen hundred square feet for our family of six. It didn't have a garage, just a shed in the back. But it was still *our* shed, with *our* stuff. One morning, as I gazed out our back kitchen window, I saw the door to that shed open. It wasn't supposed to be open. Then I noticed that the gate to our backyard was *also* open.

Someone had broken into our shed and stolen our lawn mower.

Have you ever had anything stolen? Maybe a wallet, purse, bicycle, or car? Has your house ever been burglarized? If you're like me, when it happened, I didn't just feel a sense of loss; I was angry! I felt violated, abused, and wronged. And then there was the raw economic hit we had to take as a result—we had so little that to have anything stolen was devastating.

No wonder we go to great lengths to prevent it from happening. We put locks on our doors and install security systems, turn on outside lights, and buy dogs. I heard of one house that posted a sign that said, "This property is protected by a pit bull with AIDS." Now that's subtle.

The eighth commandment talks about this kind of violation. In Exodus 20:15, God says, "You shall not steal." This command is pretty straightforward. Don't take anything from anyone or any place that isn't yours to own or take.

THREE WAYS TO ACQUIRE BY THE RULES

So how can we experience an authentic life by obeying this command? If stealing is wrong, what's right? Answer: Getting things the right way, and we can acquire things through at least three legitimate efforts.[1]

Work

First, the Bible says that we can legitimately add to our holdings by working for them. In Ephesians 4:28, the Bible says, "He who has been stealing must steal no longer, but must work, doing something useful with his own hands." Few things are more rewarding and God-honoring than laboring for the purpose of earning a living.

Investing and Trading

A second legitimate way to acquire by the rules is through skillful investing and trading. Jesus once told a story about three men who had each been given a certain sum of money. Two of the three took that money and made shrewd investments, doubling the amount that they had been given. The third man just buried what he had and did nothing with it. Jesus applauded the ones who made their money work for them and had little praise for the one who did not.

Prayer

The third approach to acquisition that the Bible affirms has to do with prayer. There are times when God gives to us in tangible ways through prayer, supplying our needs in a supernatural way. The Bible warns us never to assume that God will do this, and we should never expect God's supernatural provision to take the place of diligent labor or wise investment, but there is little doubt that our needs can be directly supplied by the hand of God.

So far, so good. God says not to steal, and He gets no dis-agreement from us. And in regard to how we *should* gain things, we can sign off on His strategies in a heartbeat. People should work for what they get, or if they can, they should gain things through honest, aboveboard investments or trades. And if God chooses to supernaturally provide for someone's needs, then good for them!

This agreement leads us to a fascinating question. If everyone agrees that stealing is wrong and that the acceptable ways of acquiring things have to do with work or investing or trading or receiving something from the loving hand of God, then why is there so much stealing in the world? Why is it that when the opportunity presents itself to get something illegally, normally law-abiding, honest citizens go for it?

In January 1997, a Brink's truck carrying 3.7 million dollars' worth of coins and currency crashed on an elevated highway in Miami, Florida. The money flew everywhere. For nearly two hours, news cameras captured the mad scramble of residents as they scooped up cash, stuffing nearly five hundred thousand dollars in bags, boxes, pants, bras—anything handy, mind you—before the police arrived on the scene and put a stop to it. To date, of the half-million taken, only around twenty dollars have been returned. An eleven-year-old boy turned in eighty-five cents that he had found, and a single mother of six who worked at a five-dollar-an-hour sales job turned in $19.53 that she had found. One man who stashed two bags of loot at home while he headed back out to the street to get more returned to find that someone had broken into his house and cleaned *him* out. Here's the irony: I'll bet if you could interview that guy, he would have said that he was violated by someone breaking into his house and robbing him, but that what *he* did in taking the money was just opportunity knocking.

Why is that?

I think it's because we all know that it's wrong when we've been stolen from, but we get a little fuzzy when it comes to having a clear understanding of what it means for *us* to steal. Let's spend a little time with this, because God did *not* say, "People should not steal." He said, "*You* should not steal." So let's take a look at three scenarios of stealing that the Bible is very specific about that might just give us an opportunity to deepen our relationship with the eighth commandment.

TAKING

The first stealing scenario has to do with taking—raw seizure. In Luke 10, Jesus tells of a man who was traveling and was jumped and beaten and robbed of all that he had. His story could have been taken from the pages of any modern newspaper. Only our opportunities have increased, evidenced by the fifty million dollars stolen by "Knightshadow," the name by which he was known to computer hackers, who stole more than one hundred thousand telephone calling-card numbers and sold them to computer hackers around the country, who in turn sold them to people overseas.[2]

In God's eyes, that kind of illicit activity is wrong. I'm sure you would agree. I doubt that you have ever been guilty of this form of stealing—at least in its more blatant manifestations. But I wonder how many of us steal in more subtle ways. Padding our expense reports, taking home pens and paper, using company supplies, running our personal letters through the office's postage meter, making long-distance personal calls, or sending faxes through corporate lines. Ready for a fast fact? It has been estimated that American businesses lose approximately forty billion dollars each year from employee theft, from pens and tools all the way up to embezzlement.[3] The practice is so widespread that the idea of it being "stealing" never appears on the radar screen. Instead, taking company supplies is viewed as more of a corporate fringe benefit.[4]

Then there's the ladder or punch bowl or tapes that you borrowed that just never got returned. Or the library books that have now become part of your collection. One hotel, in its first ten months of business, reported that it lost thirty-eight thousand spoons, eighteen hundred silver coffee pots, fifteen hundred silver finger bowls, and—get this—one hundred Bibles, which if the snatchers happen to read, will tell them that what they had engaged in was *stealing*, because it involved the taking of what was not theirs.[5]

CHEATING

The second stealing scenario has to do with cheating or any form of deception. In Proverbs 20:23, the Bible says that "God hates cheating in the marketplace; rigged scales are an outrage" (MSG). This verse is referring to a practice in which silver would be weighed on scales balanced by a stone weight. If you readjusted the scales, you could get away with giving a person less for their silver than it was really worth. God says that conscious fraud in order to cheat another person is wrong. That's important to hear, because many people today are in positions in which they are tempted to go the route of lies, half-truths, schemes, gimmicks, promotional tricks, and false advertising to turn a profit. The Bible says that these tactics are just a sophisticated way of stealing.[6]

I once took a van into a dealership to be serviced and, while I was there, asked the mechanic to check out my right electric window because the button on the driver's side no longer made it go up and down. It was an annoying but minor problem. Before leaving the dealership, I made a point to say, "But don't do *anything* to it before you tell me what it's going to cost." I even made sure the mechanic wrote my instructions down.

I got a call the next day, and a voice on the other end said,

"Well, to fix that window, we've got to replace the whole motor, and it's gonna be one hundred and seventy-five dollars."

"One hundred and seventy-five dollars!" I exclaimed. "Wow! Well, let me sit on that one for a while. It's not that big of a deal to me."

"You mean, you don't want me to do it?"

"No," I replied, "I told you that I wanted to wait and find out how much it was going to cost first."

He remembered, and then we hung up. In less than three minutes, the phone rang, and it was the mechanic again. He said, "Listen, how about if I do it for under fifty dollars? I think I made a mistake in what I told you it would cost." Suddenly, things got very clear. I don't want to perpetuate the stereotype of dishonest mechanics, but it didn't take a college degree to figure out what was going on. The guy had already done the repairs, which hadn't cost him anywhere *near* what he had originally said, and now he was stuck! If my intuitions on what was taking place behind the scenes were right, he was also a thief. False advertising, inflated costs, and telling people they need to buy something or have something done when they don't are just other forms of stealing.

DEFRAUDING

The third stealing scenario has to do with defrauding someone. This is when you withhold something from someone to whom it is rightly due.[7] It is withholding productivity and labor that are due an employer through a long lunch, running errands on company time, failing to work your full number of hours, or calling in sick when you're anything *but* sick. It's stalling a payment to a creditor so that you can go out on the town, withholding child support, or denting a car in a parking lot and driving off without leaving a phone number. Yes, defrauding even includes our relationship with the IRS. I came across the following letter that was actually sent to the agency that reflected the spirit of many: "Gentlemen: Enclosed you will find a check for $150. I cheated on my income tax return last year and have not been able to sleep ever since. If I still have trouble sleeping, I will send you the rest."[8]

THE ULTIMATE THEFT

Yet we need to take defrauding one step further and talk openly about the ultimate act of defrauding, the supreme withholding from somebody what is rightfully theirs—the human defrauding of God. Unimaginable as it might seem to defraud the One who gives life, salvation, grace, and heaven, some of us defraud God of what is His! You're probably wondering what on earth we could ever do that would result in defrauding God. In the last book of the Old Testament, the prophet Malachi records these words from God to His people:

> Will a man rob God? Surely not! And yet you have robbed me.
>
> "What do you mean? When did we ever rob you?"
>
> You have robbed me of the tithes and offerings due to me. . . . Bring all the tithes into the storehouse . . . if you do, I will open up the windows of heaven for you and pour out a blessing so great you won't have room enough to take it in!
>
> Try it! Let me prove it to you! (Mal. 3:8-10 TLB)

When people come to God—acknowledging their sins, their failures, their mistakes, and their desperate need for forgiveness—and they receive those things from God and begin a new life under His leadership, they know that nothing will ever be the same again. They lay all that they are before God and surrender the leadership of their lives to Him. God has asked them to do that, and they're delighted to do it! They know what a life without Him is like, and they know that placing everything under His control is the only way to go. From that comes the miracle of salvation and forgiveness, an altered destiny, and the beginning of God's leadership and transformational work. And as you might imagine, they are forever grateful. Next, they intuitively ask, "What can I do in return? How can I express my gratitude?" Here, paraphrasing the vast array of biblical materials that speak to the subject, is what God says:

You can respond in worship, in prayer, by joining a church, using your gifts and abilities in ministry, spreading the word of Christ to others, and altering your lifestyle under My leadership. And I want you to give full control of all of your financial resources over to Me. I want you to be free of all anxiety in that area. I will have ultimate responsibility. I want you to manage the day-by-day operation, but give Me ultimate control. And here's My first request: Take the first 10 percent of everything I send your way and give it to the church that you attend.

Can I trust you to do that?

Then, after you demonstrate faithfulness to Me in that one, simple matter, that will qualify you to move on into the adventure of resource management. I'll involve you in the adventure of giving and receiving and divesting and investing, and I'll flow resources back into your life to keep the adventure going. You'll get to be part of fascinating projects, daring rescues, and incredible answers to prayer. What I ask you to do may not make logical sense to your accountant, but one day you will gasp at My wisdom.

Are you with Me?[9]

It's kind of a three-step deal: First, you offer all of your resources to God for His control. Second, you qualify for God's involvement by being faithful with 10 percent. Third, you graduate into the lifelong adventure of giving and receiving under God's direction. Those three steps provide the gateway to one of the most dynamic, exciting, miracle-filled parts of life. Yet over the centuries, countless numbers of Christians have done the unthinkable. They have violated and frustrated God's whole economic plan. They have taken the first 10 percent that God has asked for, and they have defrauded God of that amount. They have taken what is rightfully His—what He's asked for—and they've spent it on *themselves.* They've bought toys, houses, cars, vacations, VCRs, and computers—and God feels robbed, even violated.

Let's take it even further.

You feel violated when a stranger defrauds you. Can you imagine how God must feel when one of His own adopted children, one whose very redemption cost Him the blood of Jesus, His Son—can you imagine how *He* feels when He's defrauded? He sees His children make purchase after purchase, decision after decision, and choice after choice that prevents them from giving Him what is His.

Since the heat is already turned up this high, let's get perfectly honest about why we defraud God. *We don't give God what is His because we don't trust Him.* We don't take this elemental, introductory step of authenticity and obedience because we don't trust His leadership, we don't trust that He'll provide, and we don't believe that we will be cared for. We don't buy into the fact that doing what He says is best. Even when God tells us to test Him to prove that He will provide. Look again at what He proclaimed through the prophet Malachi—isn't that what He says? "Try it! Let me prove it to you!" (3:10 TLB).

I once read of a man who was having trouble with such trust. He wanted to do the right thing, but he was finding it rough going. One day he went to a Christian friend whom he knew *had* trusted God in this area and said, "You know, I just don't see how I can give 10 percent of my income to the church when I can't even keep on top of my bills." His friend replied in a surprising way. "John, if I promise to make up the difference in your bills if you should fall short, do you think you could try tithing for just one month?"

"Are you kidding me?"

"No," he replied, "I'm not."

"Okay then, sure. If you promise to make up any shortage, I guess I could try it for a month."

Then his friend said, "John, think about what you just said. You'd be willing to put your trust in *me*—a mere man, just like yourself, who doesn't possess all that much in the world—but you can't bring yourself to trust your heavenly Father, who owns the entire universe."[10]

I don't know about you, but I need to be reminded of this more often than I care to admit. Giving God what is His and trusting Him to provide for your needs should be first place in your life, for Jesus made it first place. Remember His words? "Don't worry at all about having enough food and clothing. . . . [God] will give them to you if you give him first place in your life and live as he wants you to" (Matt. 6:31–33 TLB). The call is to trust God. So offer control of your life to Him, in honor of what you know to be true of His trustworthy character. Then bring the full tithe into the church. Because of previous choices and decisions, you may need to start with 2 percent, then 5 percent, then 8 percent, working up to the full amount. Regardless of the amount, commit to give to God, because trusting God with your money will open the door to God's involvement with your financial life. That's what the eighth commandment is after—the earning and managing of your money in a way that God can bless.

FOLLOWING OUR HEART'S DESIRE

Max Lucado writes of a letter that was sent to the U.S. government, dated February 6, 1974. It simply said, "I am sending ten dollars for blankets I stole while in World War II. My mind could not rest. Sorry I'm late." It was signed, "An ex-G.I." Then the postscript read: "I want to be ready to meet God."

He wasn't alone.

His letter is one of thousands upon thousands of letters that have been sent to the U.S. government since it began collecting and storing them since 1811. The money is put in what is called the Conscience Fund. To date, more than $3.5 million has been deposited, with tens of thousands received annually. One man wrote from Brazil, sending fifty dollars to cover the cost of two pairs of boots, two pairs of pants, one case of rations, and thirty pounds of meat he stole from the army between 1943 and 1946. A Colorado woman sent in two eight-cent stamps to make up for having used one stamp twice, which for some reason had not been canceled. A former government employee mailed in one dollar for four ballpoint pens she had never returned to the office. A man from Salem, Ohio, also sent in a dollar with the following note: "When [I was] a boy, I put a few pennies on the railroad track and the train flattened them. I also used a dime or a quarter in a silver-coating experiment in high school. I understand there is a law against defacing our money. I have not seen it but I desire to be a law-abiding citizen."[11]

Don't we all?

At the end of a speaking tour throughout England, I had arranged for four wonderful days to myself, without responsibilities, in London. I stayed in the Covent Garden area near Soho, which is the heart of London's theater district. It was there, on a cool London night, that I saw the musical rendition of Victor Hugo's *Les Misérables*.

The story revolves around Jean Valjean, a convict released on parole after nineteen years on the chain gang for nothing more than stealing a loaf of bread. The law required that as a released convict, he must display a yellow ticket of leave, condemning him to a life as an outcast. Only the saintly Bishop of Digne treats him kindly. Embittered through his years of hardship, Valjean repays the bishop's kindness by stealing his silver and escaping into the night. Valjean is caught, and the bishop's silver is found. Lying, Valjean claims the silver was a gift. The police take him to the bishop, and he awaits the words that will return him to prison for life. Yet he hears the last thing he could have imagined. The bishop confirms his story and says,

> *That is right.*
> *But my friend, you left so early*
> *Something surely slipped your mind.*
> *You forgot I gave these also*
> *Would you leave the best behind?*

And to Valjean's astonishment, the bishop hands over a pair of precious silver candlesticks. Instead of the condemnation he deserves, Jean Valjean is invaded by grace. As the constable leaves, the bishop takes Valjean aside and explains,

> *And remember this, my brother*
> *See in this some higher plan.*
> *You must use this precious silver*
> *To become an honest man.*
> *By the witness of the martyrs*
> *By the Passion and the Blood*
> *God has raised you out of darkness*
> *I have bought your soul for God!*

From that point on, Jean Valjean becomes an instrument of love and grace to those around him. His soul had been bought, and honesty was the key. But it began with an authentic life of obedience to the eighth commandment.[12]

CHAPTER 9

Telling the Truth

The Leo Burnett advertising agency did a nationwide telephone survey a few years ago on lying, cataloging *when* we lie, *how* we lie, and *why* we lie.

The results were interesting.

Ninety-one percent of all Americans confessed that they regularly lied. Seventy-nine percent had given out false phone numbers or invented new identities when meeting strangers on airplanes. One out of every five admitted that they couldn't get through even one day without going along with a previously manufactured lie. Guess what the survey revealed that we lie about the most—our income, our weight, or our age? It's our *weight!* Which is kind of funny, as that's the one truth no lie could ever conceal. In second place was money, and third was our age. There was also a contender that came in fourth: our true hair color.

Now here's what I found most intriguing about the study: People no longer seem to *care* about lying. We accept it. It doesn't bother us. We don't get upset anymore when someone exaggerates, falsifies, fabricates, or misrepresents the truth. We live in a day when we've been bombarded with erased tapes, tampered evidence, illicit cover-ups, padded résumés, and exaggerated ads—to the point that we've pretty much given up on truth being a viable enterprise. The study found that in the past, people thought lying was wrong. Now, almost half of all Americans say it isn't.[1]

And there's a simple reason why we hold to this new perspective: We've come to believe lying is *better* than telling the truth. In the film *Liar, Liar,* Jim Carrey plays an attorney who finds himself—through the answered wish of his son—unable to lie. He tries to explain to his son the importance of taking the wish back:

"Max, I got to talk to you," Carrey begins. "Your mommy told me about that wish you made last night. It came true, Max."

"Really? You mean you have to tell the truth?"

"Yes!"

"No matter what?"

"No matter what."

The son decides to test his father's newfound proclivity for telling the truth.

"Is wrestling real?"

"In the Olympics, yes. On Channel 23, no."

"Will sitting too close to the TV set make me go blind?"

"Not in a million years," his father is forced to reply.

Then, placing his fingers in his mouth with his tongue sticking out, his son asks, "If I keep making this face, will it get stuck that way?"

Drawing from real life and from the character he was playing, Carrey replies, "Uh-uh. In fact, some people make a good living that way."

"Now listen, Max," Carrey pleads. "You gotta do something for me. I need you to take back that wish."

"So you can lie?"

"Yes. But not to you! You see, Max, sometimes grownups need to lie. It's hard to explain, but if . . . look, here's a good example. When your mommy was pregnant with you, she gained a good forty pounds. There was nothing she wouldn't eat. And Daddy was scared. But when she'd ask me, 'How do I look?' I'd say, 'Honey, you look great, you're beautiful, you're glowing.' If I'd told Mommy she looked like a cow, it would have hurt her feelings. Understand?"

"My teacher tells me real beauty is on the inside."

"That's just something ugly people say. Max, no one can survive in the adult world if they have to stick to the truth. I could lose my case, I could lose my promotion, and I could even lose my job. Now I need your help, Max. Okay?"

And with a tired sigh, his son says, "Okay."

We understand, don't we? There is a sense in which we believe lying is necessary—even beneficial. And it starts young. A couple of years ago, one of my kids made a mess downstairs in our house. Most of the time, my children are pretty good about telling the truth, even when it's tough. But this time, when I got all four of them together and asked, "Okay, which one of you did it?" every one of them said, "Not me, Daddy." There I was looking at a wrecked room that I didn't wreck, my wife didn't wreck, and all four of my wonderful, beautiful little children staring at me, saying that *they* didn't wreck it *either!* Kind of like the kid with chocolate smeared all over his face, saying that he didn't eat the chocolate-chip cookies.

"Listen," I said, "one of you is not telling me the truth. Who did it?"

Same response.

Normally, that would never be the end of it. You choose your battles as a parent, and I pick mine over character. But the room wasn't that big of a deal, I wasn't really sure how it got messed up, and I was tired and in a hurry—so I did something I don't ever recall doing before. I just said, "Listen, I'm *not* going to punish you—I just want to know the truth. But if you *don't* tell me and I find out, then you'll be in *big* trouble." Instantly, one of them said, "Oh, well, if that's the deal, I did it!" Just like that! Aren't we all that way? We only tend to tell the truth when we are confident that telling a lie wouldn't be better. Truth telling becomes a kind of "take-it-or-leave-it" enterprise. It just depends on whether or not we think telling the truth will pay off.

WHERE GOD STANDS

But here's where it gets sticky. The Bible teaches us that telling the truth always pays off. In the ninth commandment, God says: "You must not lie" (Exod. 20:16 TLB). In another place, God says that He hates lying: "There are seven things that the LORD hates and

cannot tolerate: a proud look, a lying tongue, hands that kill innocent people, a mind that thinks up wicked plans, feet that hurry
off to do evil, a witness who tells one lie after another, and a man
who stirs up trouble among friends" (Prov. 6:16–19 TEV).

Of the seven things this passage says that God hates, at least two
of them have to do with lying. God hates lying because He is
truth. Truth is His very nature. So any distortion of the truth is
diametrically opposed to God and the things of God. This is why
in Ephesians, the Bible says, "Stop lying and start telling each
other the truth" (4:25 CEV).

How We Distort the Truth

Let's look at the ways that we can play with truth, because we can
be very creative.

We Can Just Plain Lie

First, we can simply say something that is not true. We can say
it's raining when it's sunny. We can say that we have a Ph.D. when
we never got out of college. We can say that we have never been
married when we have been divorced.

But it can be subtler than that.

Let's say that there is a trial. One witness says, "I saw John kill
his wife on the corner." A second person says, "I saw John on the
corner." And a third person, also a witness, doesn't say anything.
The truth is that all three saw John and know that he didn't kill
anyone. The first person just lies boldly. The second person tells

an evasive half-truth, and the third person remains in cowardly silence. All three lied, because all three tampered with the truth.[2]

We Can Distort

Second, we can distort the truth. We can misquote somebody, slander someone's reputation, make an accusation that is full of half-truths, and spread innuendo. We can tell a story a certain way in order to discredit someone or place him or her in a certain light. According to the *Chicago Tribune*, on May 9, 1994, a group of fourth graders at Fuller School on the south side of Chicago accused their substitute teacher of sexually molesting them. By evening, the story was all over the news broadcasts. The next day, police investigators interviewed fourteen of the children and determined that the charges were false. Apparently the children made up their accusation because the substitute teacher had threatened to report unruly behavior. A radio announcer reported that one child had promised to give classmates a dollar if they would join him in the lie. The teachers' union president said that exonerating the teacher doesn't always make everything better. "What usually happens when a person is accused of this kind of thing," he said, "is they're exonerated by the board publicly but then later, quietly, they're let go."[3]

Yet the two biggest distortions involve *ourselves*. The first distortion includes the things we distort in order to get something we want. When the Port Authority of New York and New Jersey ran a help-wanted advertisement for electricians with expertise at using Sontag connectors, they received 170 responses—even though

126

there is no such thing as a Sontag connector. The Authority ran the ad to find out how many applicants falsify résumés in order to get a job.[4]

The second distortion we are most tempted to pursue involves that which protects us from punishment. When my youngest son, Zachary, was three years old—but learning the ways of the world with amazing speed—he hit his older sister Rachel. He didn't see my wife, Susan, but she saw him do it. Instantly appearing in the room, she asked, "Zachary, did you hit Rachel?"

His three-year-old mind worked for a minute. "Um," he said, "*Jonathan* did it." Jonathan, his older brother, was not even in the house.

Susan pressed on. "Now, Zachary, are you telling me the truth?"

Zach's little mind whipped into action a second time, and then his older sister came to mind, and he said, "Um . . . how 'bout *Rebecca?*" He thought he'd just go down the family list until he found someone she might buy! He didn't deny that a "hit" took place; he just distorted the who, what, and where.

We Can Exaggerate

Third, we can exaggerate. We can use words like *never* and *always* in our conversations with people—you know, "You *never* do this," or "You *always* do that." We can inflate numbers and statistics. We can say we're close friends with someone we hardly know. We can pad our résumés or enlarge past accomplishments. Why do we exaggerate? Because we think the truth, by itself, is not enough.

Mack Stiles tells of a conversation he had with a man from Sweden named Andreas, who said to Mack, "I've been told if I decide to follow Jesus, He will meet my needs, and my life will get very good."

To Andreas, this was a point in Christianity's favor, and Mack was tempted to go along and make Christianity sound better than it is in order to bring his friend to faith. But he didn't.

"No, Andreas, no," Mack said. "Actually, Andreas, you may accept Jesus and find that life goes very badly for you."

"What do you mean?"

"Well, you may find that your friends reject you, you could lose your job, or your family might oppose your decision. There are a lot of bad things that may happen to you if you decide to follow Jesus. Andreas, when Jesus calls you, He calls you to go the way of the cross."

"Then why," Andreas asked, "would I want to follow Jesus?"

"Because," Mack answered, "Jesus is true."[5]

We Can Say It's Better Than the Truth.

Finally, we can lie by conveying that it's *better* than the truth. We usually call this a "white" lie, or in more recent years, a "strategic misrepresentation," "reality augmentation," or "terminological inexactitude."

This kind of lying is used in order to avoid relational conflict or an uncomfortable situation, or because it protects a person's ego or reputation in some way. They say, "You look great," when someone doesn't; "That's a good joke," when it was awful; "We'd love to come, but we're going to be out of town," when the truth is that we are *very* available but would rather have a root canal without Novocain than spend an evening with them. Most of us tell "white" lies not because they are truly of a higher "good" than the truth, but because we find them convenient or expedient. The truth is that we didn't have to lie at all.

THREE REASONS THAT GOD HATES LYING

Why is lying such a big deal to God? First, as we've already explored, the Bible teaches that God is truth. Truth is His very nature. So any distortion of the truth is diametrically opposed to God and the things of God.[6] The second reason is that lying is destructive. It hurts people. The Bible says that "a deceitful tongue crushes the spirit" (Prov. 15:4). Haven't you found that to be true? Does anything hurt more than being lied about? Is there anything more destructive to a relationship than a lie? Is there any betrayal more wounding?

There was a young man who lived during the Middle Ages who went to a monk and said, "I've sinned by telling slanderous statements about another person. What should I do now?"

The monk looked thoughtfully at the man and then replied, "Go get a chicken, pluck its feathers, and then place a feather on every doorstep in town."

So the young man did. Returning to the monk, he said, "What now?"

"Go back and pick up all of the feathers."

"But that's impossible!" he exclaimed. "How can I do that? There were hundreds and hundreds of feathers, and by now, they've blown all over town into a thousand places!"

"And that is what has happened with your lies," the wise monk answered. "The damage they have done can never be retrieved."[7]

But lying isn't just hurtful in terms of slander. It lashes out at the soul of a relationship because lying—in any form—is deceitful, and it tears away at trust. I've had the sad misfortune of helping many couples pick up the pieces after their marriage has been rocked by an extramarital affair. Time and again, it wasn't the sexual infidelity that inflicted the most damage; it was the web of lies that destroyed their foundation of relational trust.

Yet the hurt that flows from lying isn't just toward others, but toward ourselves. Think of the hurt when you tell yourself that you're a great father while your kids walk away in rebellion; that your marriage is fine, but then the divorce papers are filed; that it's always the other person's fault as you go from job to job; that you're in good shape, then the heart attack comes; that you and God are okay, then you stand before Him in judgment and come face to face with the reality of your choices. Lying to ourselves *about* ourselves is the most fundamental form of lying, and it is the most deadly, for it often involves the denying of our sins. And lying about our sins is the one sure way to stifle the work of God's grace and forgiveness, upon which our very life depends.[8] So there is a great harm that comes with lying. God knows that, so He says, "Tell the truth. Tell it to others, and at all costs, tell it to yourself."

There remains a third reason for God's concern. What is true is *real*, and what is real *matters*. Sigmund Freud was known as one of the greatest religious skeptics who ever lived, but even he agreed that believing in a lie would undermine any sense of meaning: "If it were really a matter of indifference what we believed, then we might just as well build our bridges of cardboard as of stone, or inject a tenth of a gramme of morphia into a patient instead of a hundredth, or take tear-gas as a narcotic instead of ether."[9]

A TRUTHFUL LIFE

All of us know, deep down, that a life that does not have access to the truth and does not traffic in the truth is never best. In fact, it's dangerous. But that doesn't make operating as a truthteller any easier. The temptation to lie is so strong because telling the truth can be messy. It can come with a price tag. The truth can be controversial, which is why we need help to do it. So let's take a look at how we can go about the hard work of telling the truth.

Have a Commitment to the Truth

The first step is simply to have a *commitment* to the truth. The hard work of truth telling will never be strapped on or invested in unless you have an unswerving commitment to truth *itself*. Truth will be fleshed out in your life when deep within your heart you are convinced that maintaining it is nothing less than a life standard. As Blaise Pascal observed, "Truth is so obscure in these times, and falsehood so established, that, unless we love the truth, we cannot know it."[10] We need to have an inward resolve like the psalmist who proclaimed, "I have chosen the way of truth" (Ps. 119:30).

Tell the Truth Early On

Second, start telling the truth early on. Look at what the Bible says about this: "Do any of you want to live a life that is long and good? Then watch your tongue! Keep your lips from telling lies!" (Ps. 34:12–13 NLT). Did you catch that? *Watch* your tongue; *keep* your lips from even the *start* of a lie. You know why truth telling usually gets so messy and complicated and difficult? Because we avoid telling the truth in the earliest stages; we keep letting the lies build and build until telling the truth becomes a monumental undertaking with repercussions in countless places. To make truth telling less difficult, do it in the earliest stages; practice it at the very beginning.

Be Sensitive When You Tell the Truth

Third, be sensitive to the other person when you tell the truth. One thing that makes truth telling so difficult is that we don't employ the sensitivity necessary to share truth in a positive and productive way.

The Bible tells us "we are meant to speak the truth in love" (Eph. 4:15 PHILLIPS). That's what real sensitivity is all about— speaking the truth in love. When you speak the truth *without* love, all you do is beat people up. You tell the truth, but you leave a trail of bodies behind you. There must be truth *and* love. You need to allow God to work in your life in such a way that you can communicate truth with such a kind spirit that your words become a channel for God's transforming power.[11]

The other day, my wife had to do some truth telling with me over a very sensitive issue in our marriage. We sat down, and she bravely plunged in. At first, I was a bit defensive. I was ready to do battle and win. In other words, I was barely listening to her; I was just waiting for my turn to speak. Yet she shared with me in such a loving, tender way that I was totally disarmed. I stopped waiting for my turn. I started to *hear*. When she got through, the first thing out of my mouth was, "Honey, I can't imagine anyone communicating that kind of truth to another person with more sensitivity and tenderness and love." As a result, truth was told, and truth was heard.

Earn the Right to Tell the Truth

Fourth, the waters of truth telling can be navigated with success when you *earn* the right to tell the truth to someone. Just as truth must be given with love, it must also be given in a context of trust and relationship. The truth is hard to share, but it is even harder to hear, unless someone has paid some significant relational rent.

One day a rabbi was sitting in his study when one of his students knocked on his door. The rabbi called out for the person to enter. The student entered the room, walked over to the old man's desk, and said, "I just want you to know, Rabbi, how much I love you."

The rabbi put down his book, looked over his glasses, and sensing a teaching moment, he asked, "What hurts me?"

More than just a bit puzzled, the student said, "What?"

The rabbi repeated himself. "What hurts me?"

The student was speechless. "I don't know."

"How can you love me," the old man said, "if you don't know what hurts me?"[12]

Do you see what he was after? "How can you address me intimately without knowing me? How can you say you have any sense of feeling for me and my life if you haven't walked through some of that life with me?" The greater the level of truth you share, the greater the level of intimacy there often needs to be. There was a time when Moses was leading the people of Israel, and things weren't going well. He was getting stressed, burned out, and the people were starting to grumble. Then his father-in-law, Jethro—whom Moses not only knew, but had spent forty years with in a joint partnership and relationship—came to visit. In about five minutes, Jethro sized up the situation. Then he said, "What is this you are doing for the people? . . . What you are doing is not good. . . . Listen now to me and I will give you some advice" (Exod. 18:14, 17, 19). That was hard truth, but it was shared by someone who knew Moses and had invested in Moses. As a result, look at how the Bible records Moses responding: "Moses listened to his father-in-law and did everything he said" (Exod. 18:24).

Now, just for fun, play it out another way. Let's say Moses was in the midst of his leadership weeds, but instead of Jethro coming to visit, someone whom he didn't really know, and who didn't know him, drops by and says, "Hey, Moses, you're screwing up. Let me tell you where, and how—and then what you need to do." For some reason, I don't think Moses would have responded in quite the same way. Even if what the guy advised was *exactly* what Jethro would have told him, we all know that you need to have a certain amount of relational rent paid in order to speak the truth to someone. And the deeper the truth, the deeper the relationship may need to be.

Have a Truth-Hearing Spirit

The final bit of advice the Bible would throw out in order to flesh out the ninth commandment in our life is kind of a switch from the talking side of things. It has to do with the *listening* side of things. That final bit of advice is to have a truth-hearing spirit. Someone can come to you with truth to tell—but not feel able to because of your spirit. They would be willing to venture in, even if it might get messy, but they fear you. They fear your lack of rationality, your inability to listen, or your temper. You're like a powder keg, and they don't want to set you off. This is why the Bible gives very specific advice to truth hearers: "Everyone should be quick to listen, slow to speak and slow to become angry" (James 1:19).

What would your spouse tell you, right now, if your spouse thought he or she could? If he thought you would listen and honor the fact that it is best to know, rather than to be lied to or misled? If she knew you would go through the truth with her and still be there on the other side? What truth would a child share with you that might be hard to hear but would make all the difference in the world in your relationship? What would the people who work for you or with you tell you about who they are or how they feel,

135

if they thought you would not only listen, but also extend an umbrella of grace over the conversation? What would you hear if people thought you would give truth a chance? Would they talk to you about how alcohol is destroying your life? Would they talk to you about your parenting style—a style that is destroying your children? Would they bring up something in their past—a mistake or a choice that they would give anything to go back and do over, and keeping it from you is tearing them apart—but they don't know what you would say or do? Maybe they would talk to you about the deepest, most important truth of all—that you matter to God, that you have an eternity, and that heaven's doors have been opened to you because of Christ's death on your behalf.[13]

GIFTS FROM THE RIVER

Truth telling, and truth hearing, is a difficult conversation. But it is so important. Life is short, and there are certain things we need to invest in to make this life all that God intends for it be. Truth telling is one of those things. So no matter what the truth may cost us, we will gain far more in return.

There's an old story of a poor woodcutter who worked hard to make a living for his family. Every day he would trudge into the forest with his strong, sharp ax over his shoulder. He always whistled happily as he went, because he was thinking that as long as he had his health and his ax, he could earn enough to buy all the bread his family needed. One day, he was cutting a large oak tree near the riverside. Taking a rest, he leaned his ax against the tree and turned to sit down. As he did, he tripped over an old, gnarled root, and before he could catch it, his ax slid down the bank and into the river.

"What will I do?" he cried. "I've lost my ax! How will I feed my children now?"

Just as he finished speaking, up from the lake rose a beautiful woman. She was the water fairy of the river, and she came to the surface when she heard his sad voice.

"What is your sorrow?" she asked kindly. The woodman told her about his trouble, and at once she sank beneath the surface and reappeared in a moment with an ax made of silver.

"Is this the ax you lost?" she asked.

The woodman thought of all the fine things he could buy for his children with that silver. But the ax wasn't his, so he shook his head, and answered, "My ax was only made of steel."

The water fairy laid the silver ax on the bank and sank into the river again. In a moment she rose and showed the woodman another ax. "Perhaps this one is yours?" she asked.

The woodman looked. "Oh, no!" he replied. "This one is made of gold! It's worth many times more than mine."

The water fairy laid the golden ax on the bank. Once again she sank. Up she rose. This time she held the missing ax.

"That is mine!" the woodman cried. "That is surely my old ax!"

"It is yours," said the water fairy, "and so are these other two now. They are gifts from the river, because you have told the truth."[14]

It's no fairy tale that truth is the source of many great gifts in life. Not because of a river fairy, but because of the blessing of the very hand of God.

CHAPTER 10

Being Content

I sat down and looked through some magazines this past week.

I discovered that if I want to feel right, I need to get a Nordic-Track. I don't have a NordicTrack, just a membership down at the gym, so I suddenly realized that I didn't feel as healthy as I thought I did.

I then read that if I wanted to be stylish, I would need to buy a Toyota Camry. Our family van was in the shop, so I had been driving our old Mercury Sable. That felt bad enough. Real men drive SUVs or bright red sports cars. I've got four kids, so I don't have the luxury of driving what real men drive. So I found out that I couldn't even be stylish with the cars I owned.

Then I saw that if I wanted to really *feel* the spring season, I had to *dress* for the spring season, and the only place for that was at Dillard's. I knew I wouldn't have a chance to go to Dillard's that week. Suddenly the beautiful weather just didn't seem that beautiful. I just wasn't dressed for it.

It didn't get any better. I learned that I needed to be opening my mail with a knife from Oneida. I only had a two-dollar letter opener from Office Depot. Now even my mail was disappointing. On top of that, I discovered that I couldn't have a good meal if I wasn't in Texas—at least not a meal that would satisfy me. So much for my Lean Cuisines. Then I read that if I wanted to be a man, at least a manlier man than my neighbor, I had to drive a Yard-Man mower with a Briggs and Stratton engine. At least it was cheaper than a new SUV.

I liked my house until I saw the new development's ad. I thought my family and I were close until I realized we didn't have season passes to the amusement park. I even thought I loved my wife, but since I hadn't bought her a diamond necklace from the jewelry store, I was informed that I didn't. I found out that I can't even be *romantic* with my wife unless we use Sylvania light bulbs. Wouldn't you know, we have GE.

By the time I got finished with those magazines, I wasn't just depressed—I needed counseling. Ever felt that way? We all have. It's the sad fruit of living a life that covets. No wonder it made God's top-ten list.

THE TENTH COMMANDMENT

In Exodus 20:17, God says, "You shall not covet your neighbor's house. You shall not covet your neighbor's wife, or his manservant or maidservant, his ox or donkey, or anything that belongs to your neighbor." The word *covet* is not one that we use very often anymore, but it's an interesting word. Most people think that to covet something means to want it, to desire it. That's partly true, but it's not really the whole story. Nowhere does the Bible teach that wanting something, desiring something, or having ambition for something is bad. To *covet* something means to want something that you don't have *to the point* that it so dominates your life and heart that you do not think you can be happy apart from it. If I only *had* that, if I could only *do* this, if I could only *go* there, if I could just *be* with that person—*then* I could be happy.

That's coveting.

Why It Matters

"Why is coveting such a big deal?" you may ask. "There's a lot of stuff that I want that I don't have that I *do* think would make me happy. Is that so bad?" Maybe; maybe not. Let's explore what lies behind this area of authenticity from God's perspective.

Coveting Leads to Sin

First, coveting leads to sin. Lots of sin. Coveting is an attitude, a mind-set, a disposition that is infamous for leading people to very sinful activities. Think about it. Coveting is the unrestrained desire for a particular relationship that leads to adultery. The unchecked desire for what money can bring leads to stealing. Our desire to seem bigger and more important than we are can lead us to lie. Get the picture? Coveting leads you down the road to countless choices and actions that are sinful and dishonor God.

141

Because of its insidious nature in providing the fertile ground for sins to take root, Aquinas wrote that covetousness was the root of all sins and likened it to the root of a tree, for through its roots it gives life to the plant.[1] The Bible talks very clearly about how this works in the Book of James: "We are tempted by our own desires that drag us off and trap us. Our desires make us sin, and when sin is finished with us, it leaves us dead" (1:14–15 CEV).

Like the man who went to his pastor to try to overcome his temptations: "It's like two teams of horses pullin' away at me," he explained. "One team's pullin' in one direction tryin' to get me to do what God wants, and another team's pullin' in the opposite direction tryin' to get me to do things I know God doesn't want."

"Let me ask you something," said the pastor. "Which team of horses wins?"

The man thought a moment and then realized the answer: "Whichever team I say 'giddyap' to."

Coveting Doesn't Deliver

Second, coveting will not deliver. It will not satisfy. It will not come through for us like we think it will. You'd think we'd have learned this one by now, because we start to see it when we're just little folk.

When I was in the second grade, I wanted a Johnny Rogers 500 Racing Set. It was a little round plastic track that had a matchbox-type car that you could whip around the track using a hand lever. Back then, it was a pretty fancy toy. And I wanted that racing set like nothing I've *ever* wanted. If I didn't get it for Christmas, I was just going to die.

Our family tradition was to wrap up our presents for each other and put them under the tree throughout the month of December, and then on Christmas Eve, we would open them. Christmas morning was reserved for what Santa brought. About the second week of December, I saw that my parents had put a present under the tree—from them, to me—that was shaped *exactly* like the box I saw at the store for the Johnny Rogers 500 Racing Set. But I didn't know for *sure*. Since my very life depended on it, I did the unthinkable. One afternoon, while my parents were gone and my older brother and older sister were not watching, I took my parents' present and peeled off part of the wrapping paper. But the part I peeled didn't show anything. So I peeled off a little more—just to peek, mind you, so that no one would know—but *that* didn't show anything, either. So I had to peel a little more! You smell it coming, don't you? Before I knew it, I had unwrapped my present. And it *was* a Johnny Rogers 500 Racing Set. Yes, in the second grade, with the present unwrapped, I became convinced there was a loving, benevolent God in heaven who knew my name.

Then it dawned on me. *I'd unwrapped a Christmas present.* Every kid in kid-dom knows that this is grounds for capital punishment. So, being a bright second grader, I wrapped it back up. Unfortunately, my wrapping skills in the second grade were minimal at best.

My parents came home.

I stayed in my room.

It took them a while, but pretty soon, they saw it. "James Emery White—come here!"

Uh-oh. Full name used. I knew I was in deep weeds. There wasn't time to run away, so I went in to my doom—knowing that I was going to be grounded, spanked, put in time-out, or maybe even made to do my homework. Whichever one they chose, this one was going to be bad.

But they did something worse.

"We don't think we should give you this gift."

Suddenly, my newfound faith in a loving God began to include an awareness of His justice and wrath. "No!" I shouted. "Beat me, spank me, force-feed me spinach, make me kiss my sister—anything but not give me that Johnny Rogers 500 Racing Set!"

In a moment of rare but raw child abuse, they said, "We'll see."

I lived the two weeks before Christmas not knowing whether I would be a satisfied, happy, fulfilled human being because I had gotten what I wanted, or whether I would grow up dysfunctional and warped because I was deprived of the one thing that truly mattered in life.

Christmas Eve came, and underneath the tree was my Johnny Rogers 500 Racing Set. I opened it, set it up, played with it to my heart's desire, and then . . . I got tired of it. After all, it was only a little matchbox car that went round and round a dinky little plastic track. Big deal. It was nothing compared to what I knew I wanted *next* year—a G. I. Joe Combat Bazooka!

That's the way coveting works. You want something so bad that it makes you miserable. Then you get it, and it doesn't deliver the way you thought it would. Instead of learning your lesson, you just turn your attention to something else, the next promise of satisfaction. But whatever you get, whatever you earn, whatever you accomplish, is never enough. "Bigger houses and faster cars," writes Robert Frank in his exposé of American materialism, "don't make us any happier."[2]

Coveting Cheapens Life

A third dynamic within God's command against coveting is that coveting cheapens life. Jesus was very clear about this aspect of His life mission: "I have come that they may have life, and have it to the full" (John 10:10).

Russian novelist Leo Tolstoy often told the story of a peasant who was offered all the land he could walk around in a single day. Eagerly, the man started at dawn, hurrying to get around as much as possible. The strain of his exertion began to weaken his legs, then his lungs, and finally his heart. He fell dead just as he finished his circular route, ending up with nothing. His desire for possessions was greater than his desire to live.[3] "There are people who use up their entire lives making money," observes Frederich Buechner, "so they can enjoy the lives they have entirely used up."[4]

By calling us to obey in the fight against coveting, God is calling us to see that life is found in who we *are* rather than what we *have*. As has often been stated in one form or another, the poorest man in the world is the one who always wants more than he has.

In J. K. Rowling's phenomenally popular *Harry Potter* series, the young wizard wanders accidentally into a room at Hogwarts—the school for young wizards, which holds the Mirror of Erised. Upon gazing into the mirror's reflection, Harry sees not himself, but the desires of his heart. Captivated, he returns a second night, and then a third, when he is discovered by Professor Albus Dumbledore, headmaster of the school.

"So," said Dumbledore, slipping off the desk to sit on the floor with Harry, "you, like hundreds before you, have discovered the delights of the Mirror of Erised."

"I didn't know it was called that, sir."

"But I expect you've realized by now what it does?"

"It—well—it shows me my family—"

"And it showed your friend Ron himself as head boy."

"How did you know—?"

"I don't need a cloak to become invisible," said Dumbledore gently. "Now, can you think what the Mirror of Erised shows us all?"

Harry shook his head.

"Let me explain. The happiest man on earth would be able to use the Mirror of Erised like a normal mirror, that is, he would look into it and see himself exactly as he is. Does that help?"

Harry thought. Then he said slowly, "It shows us what we want . . . whatever we want . . ."

"Yes and no," said Dumbledore quietly. "It shows us nothing more or less than the deepest, most desperate desire of our hearts. You, who have never known your

146

family, see them standing around you. Ronald Weasley, who has always been overshadowed by his brothers, sees himself standing alone, the best of all of them. However, this mirror will give us neither knowledge or truth. Men have wasted away before it, entranced by what they have seen, or been driven mad, not knowing if what it shows is real or even possible. . . . It does not do to dwell on dreams and forget to live, remember that."[5]

G. W. Target's essay "The Window" tells of two men who were confined to hospital beds in the same room. Both men were seriously ill. They developed a relationship and talked about many things—their lives, jobs, and families. The only difference between the two men was that one of them was by a window. As part of his treatment, for one hour a day, the man by the window was allowed to sit up in his bed. When he did that, he could look out and witness its view. He would describe to his roommate what he saw. In vivid terms and word pictures, he would bring the outside world to his friend. He would tell him about the beautiful park he could see, with its shimmering lake, and about the many interesting people he saw spending time there. He would tell of the games the children played below, the birds flying by, and the color of the sky.

His friend, confined to the bed, began to live for these descriptions. But after a while, he started to think that it wasn't fair that *he* wasn't by the window. Here this man got to see everything, and he could only hear about it. At first, he was ashamed of his thoughts, but he couldn't stop thinking them. His attitude got worse and worse, and it began to impact his health, and he grew increasingly ill.

One night his friend, who sometimes had difficulty with congestion and breathing, awoke with a fit of coughing and choking and wasn't able to push the button for the nurse to come to his aid. The envious man next to him just lay there, looking at the ceiling, listening to the man next to him struggle for life, choosing to do nothing.

The next day the nurse came in and found the man by the window dead.

After a proper interval, the man who was so eager to see out the window—so much that he let the man next to him die—asked if he could be moved to the other man's bed. As soon as the room was empty, he struggled up on his elbow to look out the window and fill his heart and mind with the outside world.

It was then he discovered that the window faced a brick wall.[6]

Coveting Displaces God

When you covet something that you don't have, thinking it will bring you the satisfaction and happiness you desire, you displace God. Only God can satisfy your deepest needs. Anything else is a cheap, pathetic substitute that will give momentary satisfaction at best.

John Ortberg writes that once upon a time there was a young girl whose parents took her to McDonald's. There she saw an opportunity to buy a combination of food and a little toy that

148

someone, in a fit of marketing genius, named a Happy Meal. She turned to her parents and said, "May I have it please? I must have it. I don't think I could live without it."

Her parents said, "No. The toy is a trivial little thing that just enabled the price of this package to be raised beyond what it is really worth. It's not in the budget. We can't do it." But the little girl thought to herself that they just didn't understand. They wouldn't just be buying fries, McNuggets, and a dinosaur stamp; they would be buying happiness. She was convinced that she had a little McVacuum at the core of her soul, and that her heart would be restless until it found its rest in a Happy Meal. So she said, "I want that Happy Meal more than I've ever wanted anything before. And if I get it, I'll never ask for anything again—ever. No more complaining. No more demanding. If you get me that Happy Meal, I'll be content for the rest of my life."

This seemed like a pretty good deal to her parents, so they bought it. And it worked! She grew up to be a contented, grateful, joyful woman. She lived with serenity and grace. Her life in many ways was hard: The man she married turned out to be less than the man of her dreams, abandoning her with three small children and no money. The kids were a disappointment too— they dropped out of school, sponged off of her meager resources, and eventually left without a trace. When she was an old woman, Social Security gave out, and she had to live from hand to mouth. But she never complained. She had gotten the Happy Meal. She would think of it often, saying to herself, "I remember that Happy Meal. What great joy I found there." Just as she had predicted, it had brought her lasting satisfaction. She was grateful and content the rest of her life.

Is that the way it works? We all know better, don't we? You would think that kids would catch on. But that's not what happens. In fact, the only one Happy Meals bring happiness to is McDonald's. But instead of learning this lesson, our Happy Meals just get a little more expensive.[7] Blaise Pascal once wrote that every one of us has a God-shaped hole within us. We try to fill that hole with money, relationships, toys, success, position, title, and power. We are always hoping that some new person, experience, success, relationship, or acquisition will give us a momentary easing of the insatiable, painful hunger inside and fill our soul.[8] But it doesn't happen—because it's a God-shaped hole.

THE KEY TO CONTENTMENT

So what are the keys to being content?

Know What You Truly Have

One is to simply grow in your awareness of all that you *do* have.

I'll never forget reading the economist Robert Heilbroner's walk-through of what it would take to transform the average American home into the typical dwelling of the majority of the world's inhabitants. We would have to begin by invading the house of our imaginary American family to strip it of its furniture. Everything goes: beds, chairs, tables, TV, lamps. All that can be left for the family is a few old blankets, a kitchen table, and a wooden chair. When it comes to clothing, each member of the family may keep his oldest suit or dress and one shirt or blouse. The head of the family gets a pair of shoes, but not the wife or children.

Then comes the kitchen.

All the appliances would have to come out, and the cabinets would have to be emptied. All that can stay is a box of matches, a small bag of flour, and some sugar and salt. A few moldy potatoes, already in the garbage can, have to be taken back out, for they will provide much of that night's meal. We can add a handful of onions and a dish of dried beans, but that's all. Everything else goes: meat, fresh vegetables, canned goods, any crackers or candy. All gone.

But not only do we have to strip the house this way, but we also have to dismantle the bathroom, shut off the running water, and take out all electric wires. Next, we take away the house itself. The family must move to the toolshed. Everything related to communication goes too. No more newspapers, magazines, books—not that they are missed, since we must also take away the family's literacy. Instead, all that can be left is one small radio. Then government services are removed. No more mail delivery, no more fire department. There *is* a school, but it is three miles away and consists of only two classrooms. There can't be any hospitals or doctors nearby. The nearest clinic will be ten miles away and tended by no more than a midwife. It can be reached by bicycle, provided that the family *has* a bicycle, which is unlikely.

Finally, we come to money.

The family can only be allowed a cash hoard of five dollars. That is only allowed to prevent the main breadwinner of the family from experiencing the tragedy that came upon one poor laborer who went blind because he could not raise the $3.94 that he mistakenly thought he needed to receive admission to a hospital where he could have been cured.[9]

Fill the Hole

But even gaining a perspective on all that you truly have in relation to the mass of people in the world is not enough. The only way to be truly content is to have your God-shaped hole filled by God. That's the key to contentment and the essence of obeying the tenth commandment. Jesus once had a conversation with someone about this:

A man ran up to [Jesus] and fell on his knees before him. "Good teacher," he asked, "what must I do to inherit eternal life?"

"Why do you call me good?" Jesus answered. "No one is good—except God alone. You know the commandments: 'Do not murder, do not commit adultery, do not steal, do not give false testimony, do not defraud, honor your father and mother.'"

"Teacher," he declared, "all these I have kept since I was a boy."

Jesus looked at him and loved him. "One thing you lack," he said. "Go, sell everything you have and give to the poor, and you will have treasure in heaven. Then come, follow me."

At this the man's face fell. He went away sad, because he had great wealth. (Mark 10:17–22)

This was a guy who wanted to fill the hole in his life. He comes to Jesus, calling Him a good teacher. With that one line, Jesus instantly challenges the guy to go from zero to sixty in a nanosecond. He tells him that no one is good except God, so if he thought he was really good, then he must be ready to accept that Jesus was God in human form.

Wow. Some start.

But the guy doesn't even seem to blink. He already sees in Jesus the reflection of God.

Then Jesus says, "You know the commandments—you want to be right with God, to achieve full satisfaction, go that route."

"Been there, done that," the guy replies, "and I'm empty."

Then did you notice what the text says? Jesus looked at him and *loved* him. He was a seeker, someone who wanted answers, and Jesus loved him. It's as if Jesus says, "You are so close—*so close*—and what you want is right in front of you, because what you want, what you've been searching for your whole life, is Me! I *am* good, because I *am* God! I can fill that hole in your life. But are you ready to be content? Are you ready to have Me fill the hole? Are you willing to find the answer? Your deal has been money, and you thought it would satisfy. It hasn't, so now you're trying religion, and it hasn't delivered, either.

"Now you can have the real thing—not money, not religion, but a relationship with the living God. You can follow Me—you can have the hole filled—but are you willing to stop coveting, and really see Me as the key to contentment? Here's how we'll find out—go and sell what you have and give it away—just walk away from what you were using in place of a relationship with Me, and then come, follow Me."

The interaction of Jesus and the wealthy young man reveals one of the deepest truths of human life and nature. If the soul is somehow shut off from God, "shielded from the sunshine of its eternal significance" as Ken Gire writes, it will seek significance in another place. A life designed to draw deeply from God will stretch out toward the right job, the right school, the right organizations to join, thinking if it gets enough money, enough power, enough prestige, it will satisfy its deepest longings.[10] Jesus calls the man's life to its true and only source for significance.

Then we read one of the saddest things ever recorded in the Bible. The man walked away. He couldn't let go of what he had coveted. He couldn't believe that money wouldn't somehow deliver for him more than Jesus could. He didn't understand that he had a God-shaped hole.

But you don't have to walk away.

A VISIT WITH JONI

A few years ago, I was invited to a friend's house to have lunch with a very special woman whom I have long admired from a distance—Joni Eareckson Tada. A tragic diving accident when she was a teenager left her a quadriplegic for life. When I walked into my friend's house, Joni was in the living room, in her wheelchair, being hand-fed because she doesn't have the use of her hands. She'll never be able to have children. She'll never walk, never be able to touch or feel with her hands, never be able to dress herself, comb her hair, or even embrace her husband. She's had to fight pressure sores from her wheelchair, weak shoulder muscles that come from holding up her head, back problems from having to sit in one position, and neck difficulties from constantly having to look up at people. She dreams of being able to walk a beach at sunset and feel the sand between her toes, of doing simple things like brushing her teeth, cooking, cleaning, or making up a bed. But if I had to describe Joni, I would use words like *bright, cheerful, happy, joyful, bubbly, funny*—and most importantly, *content.*

She wasn't always that way.

When her accident happened, she could not understand why God would allow such a thing to happen to her. She grew angry, bitter, and she even contemplated suicide. She couldn't face the prospect of sitting down for the rest of her life without the use of her hands, or the use of her legs. All of her hopes seemed dashed, her dreams gone. But over time, Joni began to develop a deeply personal relationship with God as a Christian. One that surprised her with its depth, meaning, and fulfillment. She began to discover what she never knew before—*joy.* And the joy came from discovering that she was a child of God, and that being in a relationship with her heavenly Father through Christ was all that she needed to be fulfilled.

Today, Joni is an internationally known mouth-artist, a talented vocalist, a radio host, an author of more than seventeen books, and an advocate for disabled persons around the world. One of the projects she leads collects old wheelchairs, then cleans them up, pumps up the tires, tightens the screws, replaces the old, worn-out parts, and then gives them to underprivileged handicapped children in Third World countries. These are children who, without Joni, would have to crawl around in the dirt because they would never be able to afford crutches, much less a wheelchair.

Joni will tell you that life is good, that God has been good to her, and that she is very content. Does she want to be healed? Of course. Does she enjoy being in a wheelchair? No! But does she think that walking is what would bring ultimate happiness? Not on your life.

One of her favorite Bible passages is from Philippians: "I have learned to be content whatever the circumstances. I know what it is to be in need, and I know what it is to have plenty. I have learned the secret of being content in any and every situation, whether well fed or hungry, whether living in plenty or in want. I can do everything through [Christ] who gives me strength" (Phil. 4:11–13).

All of the other things that we covet and make the source of our happiness won't deliver. God gave them to us for our enjoyment, but never for our satisfaction. We can be satisfied by only one thing: *God*. Joni knows that. She knows what fills the hole.[11] And that's what the tenth commandment is all about.

Maybe it's what all *ten* are about.

A Long Obedience in the Same Direction

Though Friedrich Nietzsche sought to put forth a comprehensive philosophy that would offer a complete break with Christianity, he saw with utter clarity the following spiritual truth: "The essential thing 'in heaven and earth' is . . . that there should be long obedience in the same direction; there thereby results, and has always resulted in the long run, something which has made life worth living."[1] In a book building off of this insight, Eugene Peterson spoke of Christian discipleship in terms of "a long obedience in the same direction."[2]

It's a good insight.

The truly authentic life is one in which the way we live reflects who we aim to be. We do not strive for perfection, for only one Person in human history accomplished that milestone. No, authenticity is about faithful adherence and commitment to an obedient life—not in terms of legalistic maneuvering or outward shows of religious observance, but in terms of *relationship*. Authenticity is about having the deepest needs of your life intersected by Christ and desiring to order your life around pleasing Him through obedience. As Jesus taught, "If anyone loves me, he will obey my teaching. . . . He who does not love me will not obey my teaching" (John 14:23–24). Love is at the heart of obedience. Only when we love God do we desire to live *for* God, yearn to put Him first, long to honor His name, and ache to have no other gods before Him.

And only when we love *people* do we have any yearning to live in community with *them*—community that does not result in stealing from them, lying to them, or any other activity that would war against their persons. No wonder the Ten Commandments begin and end with directives that speak so plainly to the state of our hearts—for it is only through our hearts that we can experience an obedient life. As Larry Crabb has written, "I believe it can be successfully argued that every personal or behavioral problem one might wish to change (e.g., bad temper, perverted sexual desires, depression, anxiety, overeating) results ultimately from violations of the command to love."[3]

Jesus summed up the Ten Commandments of God by saying, "'Love the Lord your God with all your heart and with all your soul and with all your mind.' This is the first and greatest commandment. And the second is like it: 'Love your neighbor as yourself.' All the Law and the Prophets hang on these two commandments" (Matt. 22:37–40). Love God and love people. Or as Augustine reflected, "Love God, and do as you please."

If you love God, you will then live a life of utter obedience. And through that, you will experience an authentic life. As Thomas Kelly wrote, "The times are too tragic, . . . man's night is too dark, the Cross is too glorious for us to live as we have lived, in anything short of holy obedience."[4]

In my own life, I keep coming back to the deep truth that spiritual authenticity is all about faithfulness. Authenticity is doing what should be done. It's about *duty*—a word seldom used anymore. I do not consider myself a particularly faithful man, but faithfulness is my life's ambition. This is why I take the commandments of God to heart. For more than anything else in this world, I want my relationship with God to be *authentic*.

Perhaps you will join me on the journey.

Notes

An Opening Word

1. Adapted from Charles Swindoll, *Come before Winter* (Portland, Oreg.: Multnomah, 1985), 119.

2. Adapted from Edward K. Rowell, ed., *Fresh Illustrations* (Grand Rapids: Baker, 1997), 147.

3. Frederich Buechner, *Whistling in the Dark* (San Francisco: Harper and Row, 1988), 90.

4. Lewis Grizzard, *Kathy Sue Loudermilk, I Love You* (Atlanta: Peachtree Publishers Ltd., 1979), 43–44.

5. Those who contend that we are no longer under law, but grace, and thereby wish to dismiss the Ten Commandments should be reminded that it is only the Old Testament ceremonial law (e.g., dietary regulations and animal sacrifices) that is now obsolete. Also, the civil law is not necessarily appropriate for modern-day nations. But the moral law was

not the law of Moses, but the law of God. To be out from under the law means to be out from under the law in regard to our justification and sanctification. But we are still under the law of God in the sense that we are under an obligation to obey it. On this, see John R.W. Stott, *Christian Basics* (Grand Rapids: Baker, 1991), 91–92.

6. On this, see Larry Crabb, *Inside Out* (Colorado Springs: NavPress, 1988), 41.

7. On this, see Philip Yancey, *The Bible Jesus Read* (Grand Rapids: Zondervan, 1999), 18. *Newsweek* magazine reported that only 49 percent of all Protestants and 44 percent of all Roman Catholics could even name four of the Ten Commandments, as cited in Bill Hybels, *Laws That Liberate* (Wheaton: Victor, 1985), 8.

Chapter 1

1. On this, see J. I. Packer, *The Ten Commandments* (Wheaton: Tyndale, 1977), 31.

2. See Lee Strobel, *Inside the Mind of Unchurched Harry and Mary* (Grand Rapids: Zondervan, 1995), 113.

3. Or as Joy Davidman put it, "Thou shalt have no other gods before me, *or in addition to me.*" See *Smoke on the Mountain* (Philadelphia: Westminster, 1953/1954), 25.

4. On this, see Hybels, *Laws That Liberate*, 13.

5. Robert Boyd Munger, *My Heart, Christ's Home* (Downers Grove: InterVarsity Press, 1954).

6. The spirit of this paragraph has been pulled from a tape given by Bill Hybels on this commandment.

Chapter 2

1. As cited by Philip Yancey, *The Jesus I Never Knew* (Grand Rapids: Zondervan, 1995), 264.

2. On this, see Hybels, *Laws That Liberate*, 23.

3. On this, see J. I. Packer, *Knowing God* (Downers Grove: InterVarsity, 1973), 38–44.

4. On this idea, see Stanley J. Grenz and Roger E. Olson, *Who Needs Theology? An Invitation to the Study of God* (Downers Grove: InterVarsity, 1996).

5. The following section has been adapted from the author's *A Search for the Spiritual: Exploring Real Christianity* (Grand Rapids: Baker, 1998), 35–42.

6. Packer, *Knowing God*, 42–43.

7. Adapted from Yancey, *What's So Amazing about Grace?* (Grand Rapids: Zondervan, 1997), 56.

8. On this, see Bill and Kathy Peel, *Where Is Moses When We Need Him?* (Nashville: Broadman and Holman, 1995), 69.

9. Adapted from Humphrey Carpenter, *The Inklings* (New York: Ballantine, 1978), 45–48, as well as my own journey to Oxford and dialogues with Oxford folk at Magdalen College and the "Eagle and Child" pub in June of 1999.

Chapter 3

1. As noted by Davidman, *Smoke on the Mountain*, 42–43.

2. Or stated positively, "Always live in awareness of God's existence." Webber's comment was drawn from Yancey, *The Bible Jesus Read*, 29.

3. Adapted from Bill and Kathy Peel, *Discover Your Destiny* (Colorado Springs: NavPress, 1996), 170.

4. Early on, the missing vowels were mistakenly assumed to create the word *Jehovah.* Closer to the actual name would be "Yahweh."

5. On this, see John Bisagno, *Positive Obedience* (Grand Rapids: Zondervan, 1979), 21.

6. The following is adapted and expanded from Hybels, *Laws That Liberate,* 33.

7. On this, see William Martin, *A Prophet with Honor: The Billy Graham Story* (New York: William Morrow, 1991), 431.

8. Adapted from R. C. Sproul, *Reason to Believe* (Grand Rapids: Zondervan, 1978), 84.

9. Adapted from David W. Dunlap, "Zoo Gift Is Revoked Because Name on Plaque Is Too Small," *New York Times,* 15 May 1997, A19.

10. Adapted from *The Best of In Other Words . . .* (Houston: Raymond McHenry, 1996), 92.

Chapter 4

1. Swindoll, *Come before Winter,* 194–95.

2. Adapted from Laura Ingalls Wilder, *Little House in the Big Woods* (New York: HarperTrophy, 1932/1959), 84–86.

3. Laura Ingalls Wilder, *Farmer Boy* (New York: Harper and Row, 1933/1961), 94.

4. Some of these aspects of workaholism have been adapted from an article in *The Baptist Standard,* 12 May 1993, 8–10.

5. For more on this idea, see Richard A. Swenson, *Margin* (Colorado Springs: NavPress, 1992).

6. This concept was drawn from Martin Moore-Ede, *The Twenty-Four-Hour Society* (Reading, Pa.: Addison-Wesley, 1993).

7. Adapted from Mark Littleton, *Escaping the Time Crunch* (Chicago: Moody, 1990), 104.

8. Nadya Labi, "Burning Out at Nine?" *Time*, 23 November 1998, 86.

9. "Breaking Point," *Newsweek*, 6 March 1995, 56–62.

10. "Demands of Game Forced Krzyzewski from Sideline," *Charlotte Observer*, 29 March 1995, B1. Fans of both Duke and Krzyzewski know that Mike has returned to his coaching position, and he now models a balanced life to many.

11. On this, see Richard A. Swenson, *The Overload Syndrome* (Colorado Springs: NavPress, 1998).

12. On this, see the discussion offered in *From Sabbath to Lord's Day: A Biblical, Historical and Theological Investigation*, ed. D. A. Carson (Grand Rapids: Academie/Zondervan, 1982), particularly the essay by A.T. Lincoln, "From Sabbath to Lord's Day: A Biblical and Theological Perspective," 343–412. The authors support first-day worship but reject sabbatarian restrictions. Early church records show a preference for worship on the "Lord's Day," but only the early church document known as the *Didache* directed Christians to meet at that time. No day was set aside in Gentile Christianity for worship until the time of Constantine and the institutionalization of the church.

What can be concluded from the biblical materials is the following: The seventh day (Saturday) was no longer regarded as a day to be especially observed by worship and rest from labor (Rom. 14:5; Gal. 4:8; Col. 2:16; Acts 15:28); the resurrection, the heart of the gospel, occurred on a Sunday; when the New Testament writers designated the various days on which the resurrected Christ appeared and spoke to His disciples, it was uniformly on a Sunday (Matt. 28:9; Luke 24:13; John 20:19); and the coming of the Holy Spirit in Acts 2 occurred on Pentecost (a Sunday). Therefore while worship on the Lord's Day (Sunday) is *descriptive* of the practice of the early church, and thus important to take note of for our practice, nowhere is it directly commanded.

13. See Davidman, *Smoke on the Mountain,* 56.

14. Ibid., 53.

Chapter 5

1. See his reflections on the invention of the Web in *Weaving the Web* (New York: HarperCollins, 1999).

2. Adapted from the recounting of the tale by Joy Davidman in *Smoke on the Mountain,* 60–61.

3. Adapted from James Dobson, *The New Dare to Discipline* (Wheaton: Tyndale, 1970/1992), 27–28.

4. Adapted from Ed Young, *Against All Odds* (Nashville: Thomas Nelson, 1992), 57–58.

5. Adapted from Jerry Vines, *Basic Bible Sermons on the Ten Commandments* (Nashville: Broadman Press, 1992), 63. I do

not know, however, whether these stages are original with Dr. Vines.

6. Bruce Springsteen, ASCAP, 1989.

Chapter 6

1. Abraham Heschel, *Who Is Man?* (Stanford: Stanford University Press, 1965), 24.

2. Ann Tusa and John Tusa, *The Nuremberg Trial* (New York: Atheneum, 1984), 167. Acknowledgments to Ken Gire for alerting me to the sources used within this paragraph through his book *The Reflective Life* (Wheaton: Victor, 1998), 33.

3. C. S. Lewis, *The Weight of Glory* (New York: Macmillan/ Collier, 1949), 19. This was taken from a sermon titled "The Weight of Glory" at Solemn Evensong in the twelfth-century Oxford University Church of St. Mary the Virgin on June 8, 1941.

4. Adapted from Philip Yancey's recounting of the film's scene in *What's So Amazing about Grace?* 280.

5. The most common word for "kill" in the ancient Hebrew language was *haraq*. In the sixth commandment, the word used is *ratsakh*, which refers specifically to murder, but interestingly, never to the killing that would take place in war.

6. On this, see Packer, *The Ten Commandments*, 51–52.

7. Adapted from Shawn Pogatchnik, "Book Takes N. Ireland's Blood Toll," *Charlotte Observer*, 9 October 1999, 16A.

8. For a discussion of the various ways to commit murder beyond homicide, see Packer, *The Ten Commandments*, 52–53.

9. On this, see Gilbert Meilaender, *Bioethics: A Primer for Christians* (Grand Rapids: Eerdmans, 1996), 58.

10. Robert Schwarzwalder, "Bioethicist Offers Deadly 'Solution' to Human Frailty," *Charlotte Observer*, 5 July 1999, 11A.

11. There are a number of books that help Christians grapple with the many complex issues surrounding bioethics. For an excellent introduction, see the previously cited book by Gilbert Meilaender, *Bioethics: A Primer for Christians.*

12. Adapted from Rowell, *Fresh Illustrations*, 24.

13. Adapted from Craig Brian Larson, ed., *Contemporary Illustrations* (Grand Rapids: Baker, 1996), 144.

14. On this, see George Weigel, *Witness to Hope: The Biography of Pope John Paul II* (New York: HarperCollins, 1999), 46ff, 756ff.

15. In no way should the exploration of "second-degree" murder in the context of this commandment be fully equated with first-degree murder. This runs the risk of eisegesis and can water down the meaning of the word *murder* itself. On this, see Davidman, *Smoke on the Mountain*, 77–78.

16. Will D. Campbell, *Brother to a Dragonfly* (New York: Continuum, 1987), 181.

17. On this, see Hybels, *Laws That Liberate*, 74.

18. From Harold J. Sala, *Heroes* (Uhrichsville, Ohio: Promise Press, 1998), 205.

19. Adapted from Robert Fulghum, *All I Really Need to Know I Learned in Kindergarten* (New York: Villard Books, 1989), 19–20.

20. See *Charlotte Observer*, 16 December 1993.

21. "2,031 Offer Marrow to Help Girl, 4" *Charlotte Observer*, 1 February 1997, B1.

Chapter 7

1. See Dr. Lana Staheli, *Triangles* (New York: HarperCollins, 1997) xiii.

2. Eric Tisdale, "My Girlfriend's Father—What a Man!," *Glamour*, June 1998; as cited by Wendy Shalit, *A Return to Modesty* (New York: The Free Press, 1999), 194.

3. Adapted from Swindoll, *Come before Winter*, 49.

4. On this, see J. Allan Petersen, *The Myth of the Greener Grass*, rev. ed. (Wheaton: Tyndale, 1991), 8.

5. "Adultery: A New Furor over an Old Sin," *Newsweek*, 30 September 1996, 56.

6. Staheli, *Triangles*, 106.

7. This story comes from Alfred Ells, *Restoring Innocence: Healing the Memories That Hinder Sexual Intimacy* (Nashville: Thomas Nelson, 1990) 31–36.

8. Though it can be found in Dr. James Dobson's book *Straight Talk to Men and Their Wives* (Waco: Word, 1980), particularly the chapter "A Man and the Straight Life," I've adapted this material more from Dobson's live presentation of it in the original "Focus on the Family" film series, now available

through the video "What Wives Wish Their Husbands Knew about Women" (Word LifeWare Video).

9. Staheli, *Triangles*, xiv.

10. As noted by Peel, *Where Is Moses When We Need Him?* 177.

11. David Ireland, *Letters to an Unborn Child* (New York: Harper and Row, 1974), 33–34.

Chapter 8

1. These three are outlined by Bill Hybels in *Laws That Liberate*, 94–95.

2. "MCI Worker Is Charged in Huge Phone-Card Theft," *Chicago Tribune*, 4 October 1994.

3. As noted by Peel, *Where Is Moses When We Need Him?* 189.

4. As noted by Ross Marks, *Be My People: Sermons on the Ten Commandments* (Nashville: Abingdon Press, 1991), 76.

5. As cited by Jay W. Marshall, *The Ten Commandments and Christian Community* (Scottdale, Pa.: Herald Press, 1996), 88.

6. See Hybels, *Laws That Liberate,* 101.

7. Ibid., 102.

8. This letter, actually received by the IRS, is reprinted from Swindoll, *Come before Winter,* 91.

9. Adapted from a similar free-flowing paraphrase based on the biblical materials given by Bill Hybels.

10. Adapted from James S. Hewett, ed., *Illustrations Unlimited* (Wheaton: Tyndale, 1988), 461–62.

11. This section adapted from Max Lucado, *Six Hours One Friday* (Portland, Oreg.:Multnomah, 1989), 81–85.

12. The musical *Les Misérables* is based on the novel by Victor Hugo. The quoted dialogue comes from the musical by Alain Boublil and Claude-Michel Schonberg. The music itself was by Claude-Michel Schonberg, with lyrics by Herbert Kretzmer. The original French text was by Alain Boublil and Jean-Marc Natel, with additional material by James Fenton. All songs published by Alain Boublil Music Ltd.

Chapter 9

1. Bernice Kanner, "Unlike George Washington, Most Americans Can Tell a Lie," *The (Louisville, Ky) Courier-Journal,* 4 June 1996, C5.

2. Adapted from Davidman, *Smoke on the Mountain,* 107–8.

3. Adapted from Jacquelyn Heard and William Recktenwald, "Teachers Union Springs to the Defense of Exonerated Substitute," *Chicago Tribune,* 18 May 1994, sec. 2, p. 5; and *Chicago Tribune Magazine,* 1 January 1995, 16.

4. As reported by Peter LeVine in *Boardroom Reports,* 5 July 1993. Adapted from Rowell, *Fresh Illustrations,* 143.

5. Adapted from J. Mack Stiles, "Ready to Answer," *Discipleship Journal,* March/April 1997, 42–43.

6. On God's truthfulness, see Titus 1:2; Numbers 23:19; 1 Samuel 15:29.

7. Adapted from Michael P. Green, ed., *Illustrations for Biblical Preaching* (Grand Rapids: Baker, 1982, 1985, 1989), 175.

8. As noted by Davidman, *Smoke on the Mountain*, 112.

9. As quoted in Robert Maynard Hutchins, ed., *Great Books of the Western World*, vol. 3, The Great Ideas: II (Chicago: Encyclopedia Britannica Inc., 1982), 915. On the idea of truth in Christian thought, see the author's *What Is Truth?* (Nashville: Broadman and Holman, 1994).

10. Pascal, *Pensees*, XIV, trans. W. F. Trotter, (New York: E. P. Dutton & Co., Inc, n.d.), 864.

11. As noted by Bill Hybels, *Making Life Work* (Downers Grove: InterVarsity Press, 1998), 95.

12. Gire, *The Reflective Life*, 134.

13. Some of these questions were adapted from Hybels, *Making Life Work*, 90–91.

14. Adapted from "The Honest Woodman," in *The Book of Virtues*, ed. William J. Bennett (New York: Simon and Schuster, 1993), 602–3. *The Book of Virtues* version is itself an adaption from Emilie Poulsson, based on the poem by Jean de La Fontaine (1621–1695).

Chapter 10

1. Aquinas, *Summa Theologica*, I–II, 84, 1.

2. Robert H. Frank, *Luxury Fever: Why Money Fails to Satisfy in an Era of Excess* (New York: The Free Press, 1999), 6.

3. Adapted from the retelling by John Bisagno, *Positive Obedience* (Grand Rapids: Zondervan, 1979), 73.

4. Buechner, *Whistling in the Dark*, 80.

5. J. K. Rowling, *Harry Potter and the Sorcerer's Stone* (New York: Arthur A. Levine Books/Scholastic Press, 1997), 213–14. Some Christians have raised concerns about the Harry Potter books, most notably regarding the use of magic and the presence of certain "dark" themes and even violence. Yet the magic used in the books is mechanical, not from the occult. There is no contact with the supernatural world (at least through the first three books of the series). The overarching theme is the fight between good and evil, and that evil is real and must be resisted. Further, the characters develop courage, loyalty, and willingness toward self-sacrifice. The mechanical magic in the Rowling books should be contrasted with the real-life witchcraft the Bible condemns, which encourages involvement with supernatural evil. I would tend to categorize the Harry Potter books with the fantasy works of Lewis and Tolkien, in which wizards and witches and magical potions also abound, but in a Christian framework by which the author uses them to present good as good, and evil as evil.

6. Adapted from G. W. Target's essay, "The Window," *The Window and Other Essays* (Mountain View, Calif.: Pacific Press Publishing Association, 1973), 5–7.

7. Adapted from John Ortberg, *Love Beyond Reason* (Grand Rapids: Zondervan, 1998), 91–93.

8. Blaise Pascal, quoted in Peel, *Ten Commandments*, 224.

9. Adapted from Ron Sider, *Rich Christians in an Age of Hunger* (Downers Grove: InterVarsity Press, 1977). Heilbroner's essay is, no doubt, in need of an update since its original detailing, but its contours remain depressingly accurate.

10. On this, see Ken Gire, *Windows of the Soul* (Grand Rapids: Zondervan, 1996), 49.

11. Joni has written a biography of her life, simply titled *Joni* (New York: Bantam, 1976).

A Final Word

1. Friedrich Nietzsche, *Beyond Good and Evil,* trans. Helen Zimmern (London: 1907), sec. 188, 106–9, quoted in Eugene Peterson, *A Long Obedience in the Same Direction* (Downers Grove: InterVarsity, 1980), 13.

2. Peterson, *A Long Obedience.*

3. Larry Crabb, *Inside Out* (Colorado Springs: NavPress, 1988), 43.

4. Thomas R. Kelly, *A Testament of Devotion* (New York: Harper and Row, 1941), 72.